Week
Loan

STUDYING SOCIETY

Studying Society

An Introduction to Social Science

G. B. J. ATKINSON
B. McCARTHY
K. M. PHILLIPS

OXFORD UNIVERSITY PRESS
1987

Oxford University Press, Walton Street, Oxford OX2 6DP

Oxford New York Toronto
Delhi Bombay Calcutta Madras Karachi
Petaling Jaya Singapore Hong Kong Tokyo
Nairobi Dar es Salaam Cape Town
Melbourne Auckland.

and associated companies in
Beirut Berlin Ibadan Nicosia

Oxford is a trade mark of Oxford University Press

Published in the United States
by Oxford University Press, New York

British Library Cataloguing in Publication Data

Atkinson, G. B. J.
Studying society: an introduction to social science.
1. Social sciences
I. Title II. McCarthy, B.
III. Phillips, K. M.
300 H85

ISBN 0-19-878013-3
ISBN 0-19-878012-5 Pbk

Library of Congress Cataloging in Publication Data

Atkinson, G. B. J.
Studying society.
Includes index.
1. Social sciences. 2. Sociology. I. McCarthy, B. (Barry) II. Phillips, K. M. (Kenneth M.)
III. Title. H61.A85 1987   301   86-33247

ISBN 0-19-878013-3
ISBN 0-19-878012-5 (pbk.)

Set by Colset Private Limited, Singapore
Printed in Great Britain
at the University Printing House, Oxford
by David Stanford
Printer to the University

Preface

More than any other branch of study, social science is about the everyday life of people. Amazingly, the majority of people live their lives with only the most rudimentary and unquestioning understanding of the social forces which shape and determine them. Some might argue that it is better left that way—the more we know about these forces the more discontented we might become. But there have always been those who have wanted to know more either from a detached scientific interest in understanding what it is that makes human societies work or from a belief that greater understanding might help to show the way in which people's lives can be improved. As societies have become more developed time for such intellectual inquiry has grown. And as societies have become more complex economically, politically, and technologically then the imperative for this greater understanding has assumed an ever growing importance.

Thus social science brings together those who, for whatever reason, wish to know more about people and the social forces which shape and determine their lives. This book has been written to introduce the reader to the contribution that social science can give to these matters. But first a word of warning. Social science may require you to step outside of everyday assumptions and relationships in order to look at them in more detail and perhaps to begin to question them quite critically. The acquisition of new knowledge and understandings can be painful. But this too is the great excitement of social science and from it comes the enormous reward of being freed from unquestioned prejudices and limited ideas. Social science opens up a whole host of alternative perspectives about society and awareness of the great complexities and variations in social arrangements that exist today and have done so in the past. There can surely be no greater or more worthwhile endeavour for human beings than to understand their fellow beings better. Our hope is that after reading this book you will wish to take part in this endeavour, to go deeper into some of the issues we have touched on, and to consider the many others we have not been able to mention.

In order to make this a truly introductory book to the broad area of social science we have rejected the idea of simply presenting separate descriptive accounts of the individual disciplines which make up social science. Instead we have chosen first of all to take four of the major dimensions into which people's lives can be divided—as workers, participants in politics, members of a family, and as friends and acquaintances. The examination of these dimensions allows us to show how the separate social science disciplines have a shared contribution to make towards a greater understanding of them.

We have not tried to give complete coverage of these dimensions. Instead we have taken a few of the numerous issues of interest to social scientists that arise from each of these dimensions. We ask, for example, Why do people work? and Why do people become friends? In looking at these issues we hope not only to provide the reader with some useful information but also to illustrate how social scientists—of whatever discipline—go about the job of researching and analysing their subject.

The four dimensions of people's lives and the issues within them that are looked at in some detail have been chosen because they facilitate the introduction of many of the *concepts* and *methods* that are central to social science as a whole. They also allow for the reader to be introduced, by means of *profiles*, to some of the individual social scientists who have made a significant contribution to the general field of social science. In addition, occasional use has been made of fairly lengthy quotations (sometimes numerical), referred to as *documents*, from these and other social scientists in order to give the reader a flavour of the style and content of social science writing.

In presenting this material on the central concepts and methods of social science, the profiles of individual social scientists, and documents from social science writing, we have adopted the technique of separating them from the text by means of 'boxes' which are individually numbered. A full list of these under the headings of 'Concept Boxes', 'Method Boxes', 'Profiles', and 'Documents' is included after the Contents page at the beginning of the book. The adoption of this strategy of presenting information on these matters provides the reader with a choice of a variety of routes through the book. It can be read cover to cover, or considered from any one or more of the central themes of concepts, methods, profiles, or documents. Finally, this form of presentation makes the book into a lasting source of reference for those who we hope go further in their reading and study of social science.

In the final analysis, the major factor which unites social science is the existence of a range of methods of study which are widely used by its practitioners regardless of the particular discipline to which they belong. The use of these methods also raises issues—referred to here as methodological issues—which are of common concern to all social scientists. The methods used by social scientists and the issues raised about them are often underplayed in introductory books because of their complexity, but in this book they are given prominence. Indeed, the emphasis on them provides the third strand to our claim to offer a comprehensive introduction to social science as a whole.

The methodological issues that underlie their use and which help to unify social science are considered in some detail in the introductory and concluding chapters. These methodological issues can be most easily grasped by contrasting the approach of the social scientist to the 'man in the street' and this is done in the first chapter where 'race relations' is taken as the topic to illustrate the contrasts. We are aware, however, of the limitations of social science. Thus while the first chapter stresses the limits of everyday thinking, the final one stresses the limits of social science itself.

We hope that readers will be encouraged to pursue their interest in social science and if they do finally specialize in one of its constituent disciplines we hope that they will remain conscious of the important contribution that all the social science disciplines can make to the study of society and the individuals, groups, and institutions of which it is composed.

In writing this book we have had the help and advice of a number of people, but we would like to pay special tribute to Stewart Brooks whose ideas have done so much to shape our thinking and to the librarians of Lancashire Polytechnic who provide such a marvellous service.

We should also like to thank the following copyright holders for permission to reproduce material: M. Banton and the Tavistock Press, Z. Layton-Henry and Allen & Unwin, *The Sunday Times* for two extracts, E. J. Kolb, Prentice Hall, and Penguin Books for an extract from Margaret Mead.

Contents

Concept Boxes

Profiles

Method Boxes

Documents

Figures and Tables

1 Race Relations and The Limits of Everyday Thinking

... the social sciences study men living in society. (Duverger 1964, p. 11)

... the systematic study of man's social life. (Finnegan 1981, p. 8)

... the application of scientific methods to the study of the intricate and complex network of human relationships and the forms of organisation designed to enable people to live together in societies. (Mitchell 1968, p. 178)

Despite the apparent differences between these and numerous other possible definitions of 'social science', they all at least agree that it is about people. Clearly, though, social science is not concerned with every single aspect of human beings. For example, social scientists are not particularly interested in the purely biological aspects of life. How much blood does the human body contain? At what rate do bodies decompose? How long can people live without food and water? Social scientists are quite content to leave questions such as these to others. Physicians can specialize in the blood-and-guts aspects of life, but even they have need on occasion for the work of the social scientist. Physicians have of necessity to relate to their patients and need to be aware of the social influences on themselves and their patients not least on such matters as attitudes toward health and access to it. The social scientist's interest in people therefore emphasizes their relationships and in particular how these relationships fit into and are affected by the way society is structured into such things as groups, institutions, and broader categories like gender, class, and 'race'. This interest may be limited to a particular time or to changes over different time periods.

Social science is different from other areas of study because both those who work in this field—the social scientists themselves—and their subject-matter are the same. Both social scientist and subject are people. As a result the individuals who make up the subject-matter of the social scientists already hold information and opinions about most of the issues with which social socientists are concerned. Everybody knows something about people and their relationships. That is why some critics seem to believe that social scientists do nothing except say in complicated ways what everybody already knows. That view is sometimes true—social scientists can and do write rubbish. But it is not the whole truth. Social science can change your life because it can change the way you think and see the world. It can have this dramatic affect because social science has developed a way of looking at the world that is often in marked contrast to the way ordinary people view it.

There is a marked difference then between the approach of the social scientist to the study of human relationships and that of the ordinary person. We can call the latter 'everyday thinking'. The bulk of this chapter is concerned with exploring the characteristics of the social science approach as it contrasts with that of 'everyday thinking'. Throughout, examples of both approaches will be compared.

Everyday thinking can be valuable. Much of the social scientist's subject-matter consists of information about people and the opinions they hold. Often social scientists are able to show that commonly accepted viewpoints are correct. Significantly, at other times social science questions everyday views and calls for drastic rethinking. In making critical comparisons with everyday thinking we do not claim that the social science approach is above criticism. Indeed the final chapter will subject social science thinking to a similar critical test to that which is applied here to everyday thinking.

In order to highlight the key characteristics of the social science approach, the discussion which follows focuses on one area of human relationships, that of 'race relations'. This is a good topic for our purposes because it is something with which ordinary people are deeply concerned and about which they hold strong views. As a subject within social science, race relations has attracted the attention of each of the disciplines which make up the social sciences yet at the same time it is an example of an area which lends itself to an interdisciplinary approach. What these constituent disciplines are and what is meant by an interdisciplinary approach are considered later on in this chapter.

We begin the comparison of everyday and social science thinking by reproducing a number of quotations which approximate to some of the everyday thinking on race relations. The views recorded here are not meant to be representative nor are they necessarily widely held. Their sole purpose is to allow us to make contrasts between them and the key characteristics of the social science approach to the same issues.

Examples of Everyday Thinking

(1) Reply of a man questioned about attacks on black people by a gang of youths:

'Well, it's out of order isn't it? Everyone's entitled to live, you know, you know, there's a little bit of racial in everyone, but there you go. Especially if we're sort of, we're inundated with them, ain't we, it's getting overcrowded. I mean, you've got to admit even the housing problem's enough, isn't it?' (Husband 1982, p. 193)

(2) Letter to *Leicester Mercury* 7 May 1976 following national coverage of a case whereby two homeless Asian families arriving from Malawi were given accommodation in a four star hotel by West Sussex County Council:

'My wife has just had a major operation, and will not be able to work again for six months. She sent in her sick note and the social service office wrote back saying she was out of benefit and would not receive any allowance. If this is the case, what benefit have these Asians got in to claim £600 a week hotel allowance. I say help your own countrymen before others and I think most of your readers will agree.'

(3) Statement from the Southall Residents' Association 1963:

'The residents saw their whole life threatened and endangered by a flood of immigrants who were generally illiterate, dirty and completely unsuited and unused to our way of life. They overcrowded their properties to an alarming degree, create slums, endanger public health and subject their neighbours to a life of misery, annoyance, abuse and bitterness. . . .' (Troyna 1981, p. 25)

(4) Respondents in a social survey:

(a) 'It's like a pedigree dog. English is a pedigree. French is a pedigree.

German is a pedigree. You get an Englishman marrying a coloured he's lost his pedigree, like you get an alsatian put to stud with a dalmatian, you ain't got a pure bred anymore. It's gone, hasn't it?' (White person)

(b) 'A minority are friendly: when you say the majority, you don't know what they are thinking underneath. They are cursing you around the back.' (West Indian person)

(c) 'The immigrants already in the country are having families and they're growing up and having families. By the turn of the century, I can see us being two-thirds immigrant, counting the European immigrants . . . and by the middle of the next century, I can see the country virtually losing its national identity.' (White person) (Community Relations Commission 1976, pp. 22, 23, 38)

(5) Speech by Enoch Powell, MP:

'From whole areas the indigenous population, the people of England, who fondly imagine that this is their country and these are their home-towns, have been dislodged—I have deliberately chosen the most neut-ral word that I could find . . .

My judgement then is this: the people of England will not endure it. If so, it is idle to argue whether they ought or ought not to. I do not believe it is in human nature that a country, and a country such as ours, should passively watch the transformation of whole areas which lie at the heart of it into alien territory.' (Smithies and Fiddick 1969, pp. 73-4)

Although we have emphasized that these quotations are not meant to be representative of everyday opinion on race relations, most people would agree that the sentiments and ideas presented in them are com-monly found in British society today. Indeed, with a minimum of translation they might be applied to racial minorities in many other countries. As we shall see they contrast sharply with the writing of social scientists on the same subject.

Characteristics of Social Science

Five broadly defining characteristics of the social science approach are introduced in this chapter. Some of them are more fully exam-ined in later chapters in the book. Each characteristic will be illustrated by means of a quotation from a piece of social science writing on race relations and immigration. The same strategy will be used towards the end of the chapter in order to explain differences between the various disciplines which make up social science. By the end of the chapter, therefore, a considerable range of social science writing by some of the notable scholars in the field of race relations will have been sampled. As well as gaining familiarity with the style and specialized vocabulary of social science writing you should gain a useful introduction to the social science understanding of race relations.

Method Box 1.1 Characteristics of Social Science

It is possible to discuss the characteristics of social science in many different ways. In essence the features that distinguish social science are broadly comparable to those for all sciences. We have concentrated on five:

(1) The search for objectivity.
(2) An awareness of the complexity of social issues.
(3) Care and definition in the use of terms, i.e. conceptualization.
(4) An attempt to build theories.
(5) Methodological rigour.

The foremost characteristic that helps to distinguish social science from everyday thinking on social issues like immigration and race relations is the search for objectivity. The following passage by an economist writing about race relations illustrates this:

At the present time, questions of immigration and race relations are highly controversial, or at least touch a number of raw nerves.

Thus an economist who examines these questions faces a dilemma. Should he try to confine himself to 'objective' facts and analysis, excluding value-judgements, or should he make his value-judgements quite explicit? This is a question examined by Professor Gunnar Myrdal in his classic study of the race problem in the USA. His conclusion is that complete objectivity is probably impossible: one's value-judgements are likely to influence, for example, the kind of question one examines. The best course is to make one's value-judgements explicit, so that readers can take account of them. This view is not shared by all social scientists, but it is one to which I subscribe. Although it is highly desirable to examine migration questions in a factual, analytical manner, we ought to recognise that value-judgements are inextricably involved; in most cases, academics who purport to be purely scientific either have nothing useful to say or have unconsciously incorporated value-judgements into their analysis. (Hallett 1970, p. 441)

The idea of objectivity is examined more fully in chapter 4, but at this stage it is important to emphasize that it can rarely be achieved, not least because social scientists are themselves products of the societies they study. Like other people they will have absorbed and developed personal values and beliefs about the behaviour of people and the workings of society. They can never divorce these entirely from their work. Their values and beliefs will affect which issues they are interested in, the selection of evidence, the adoption of research strategies, and the interpretations they give to their findings. We shall consider this issue later when we look at a range of perspectives which distinguish between the different approaches that social scientists can take to their work. Many social scientists acknowledge, therefore, the need to make clear their personal values so that their affect can be taken into account by those reading their work.

The search for objectivity, even if it cannot be totally successful, still contrasts sharply with the more subjective and unconsciously value-laden nature of most everyday thinking. The latter often does not include a recognition of this factor nor even admit that it is problematic. The lack of objectivity can be seen if we analyse people's thinking. In the examples of everyday thinking that were given earlier the following terms and ideas were expressed: *inundated* with them; help your *own countrymen* before others; whole way of life *threatened* and *endangered* by a *flood* of immigrants; *people of England* . . . have been *dislodged*; *alien territory*. These emotive phrases printed in italics show the bias and lack of objectivity of the speakers.

The second distinctive feature of the social science approach can be summed up as *an awareness of the complexity of social issues*. This contrasts with the relative over-simplification commonly found in everyday approaches. Consider the following piece of social science writing:

Immigration has brought sucessive flows of individuals and families to various destinations in London, the Midlands, and the North. Most were attracted by opportunity; some were refugees. They vary in the length of their settlement, in their family structures, in their skills and economic activity, in their culture and in their faith. Above all, their diversity of origin—national, regional, island—is often maintained through distinctions that most policy makers are accustomed to obliterate with such generalities as 'Asian' or 'West Indian' or with such shorthand or blanket terms as 'immigrant', 'New Commonwealth' or 'ethnic minority'. Yet if a diversity of origins and culture defies such general categories, there are still common factors, above all, the common threat of racism and discrimination and widespread (but by no means universal) material disadvantage. To this extent diverse minority groups share some common circumstances and this convergence underlies the increasing prevalence of such general terms as 'black' or 'black British', which emphasizes the distinctiveness of colour in a white society. (Young and Connelly 1981, pp. 1–2)

The social scientists who wrote this passage felt it necessary to emphasize the complex differences between the many groups and individuals who make up those referred to as immigrants. They note that there are many differences between ethnic groups in terms of such things as place of settlement, length of residence, family structures, skills, economic activity, culture, and religion. Our examples of everyday thinking, on the other hand, ignored the diversity of the immigrant population by the use of such blanket terms and phrases such as 'them', 'these Asians', 'immigrants', and 'coloureds'.

The awareness of complexity that characterizes social science is particularly important when we try to analyse causes. In everyday thinking people often put forward just one cause like 'people are unemployed because they are lazy' or 'it's all the government's fault'. In contrast, the social scientist's recognition of the complexity of most social issues means that they need to be explained by a whole variety of causes. One of the hardest tasks of the social scientist is to disentangle causal factors, assign priorities between them, and determine the nature of the effect that they have.

In the popular mind cause and result often seem to be related in a simple and obvious way. Thus in one of the everyday quotations given above a direct causal relationship is seen between immigration and the housing problem, and the creation of slums in particular. In everyday life if two things are found together then it is often taken for granted that one causes the other. If I forget about the cake in the oven and then find it burnt black, it is easy to determine cause and effect. For social issues this relationship is much less clear. When workers go on strike they may say it is for more pay, but the underlying reasons may be that work is boring, the conditions dreadful, and the management petty. Similarily, immigrants are often found in areas of poor housing and this leads some people to believe that immigrants *cause* poor housing. An alternative explanation is that the original inhabitants moved out as conditions worsened or because their circumstances improved. They left vacant premises for newcomers who were immigrants who perhaps for economic reasons and/or prejudice were denied housing elsewhere. Other explanations are possible: for example, landlords may exploit immigrants by refusing to do repairs because they believe that they will not know their legal rights. It may well be that immigration and the housing situation are *independent* of each other even though they are associated together in the popular mind. (By 'independent' here, we mean that they may not be directly linked but affected instead by some other external factors.) Immigration and housing provide a good illustration of a social issue where the conclusions of social science are diametrically opposed to everyday thinking. As one group of researchers has put it, the migrant 'is not the author of the city's housing problem, but he is only too likely to be made the scapegoat for it' (Rose 1969, p. 248).

A recognition of the complexity of social issues leads directly to the third characteristics of social science which emphasizes that great care has to be taken in the definition and use of terms. We will refer to this as *conceptualization* for short. This characteristic can be demonstrated most vividly by considering the term 'race' itself. In everyday speech the term is used very loosely and in most cases the users of the term would have considerable difficulty defining what they mean by it. 'Race' is a key concept to many social scientists but even so there is still considerable doubt about its usefulness because it is possible to argue that separate races do not exist.

Concept Box 1.1 Race

Of all the concepts considered in this book, that of race is the most complex and controversial. It is widely used in everyday discourse, is officially recognized in such legislation as the Race Relations Act, and the study of race relations is an important aspect of social science. The complexity arises in part because the concept was originally a biological one but it has been adopted as a sociological and cultural term for distinguishing between different groups of people.

The controversy arises because it is now accepted that the idea of being able to divide people into biological races is invalid. This is made clear from the following quotation from an authorative study by Unesco:

A moderate conclusion is that despite the shortage of historical-biological data about the earlier periods of human existence, it is clear that broad categories of mankind can be distinguished on the basis of appearance and blood groupings, but that there has been so much mixture of races, and therefore so much modifiability of these physical qualities, that it is of little use in understanding human behaviour or history to analyse them in terms of physical race. Humans have shown extraordinary adaption to their physical environment, and an insatiable desire to migrate, and the progress made by man, in any field, seems to have been increasingly, if not exclusively, based on culture and not the transmission of genetic endowment.

If the concept of biological race is invalid so too must be the idea that the assumed physical characteristics of races accord with different social and cultural characteristics. This is what the Unesco study referred to as 'the transmission of genetic endowment'. In social science the alternative term of ethnic groups has now been adopted to discuss groups of people differentiated in terms of social and cultural arrangements and thereby using a term free from any inference that such arrangements are biologically determined. In terms of the physical and social sciences the concept of race should now be assigned to the dustbin of history. But the concept lives on and still exerts a considerable force in people's minds and continues to feed the myths once associated with it. One social scientist has concluded:

Regardless of the scientific opinion that there are no valid grounds to attribute to race any serious role in human history, racial beliefs are nevertheless real to many men and women, and mythical beliefs about race are commonly held. The two great persistent myths are that race and culture are directly related, and that some races are intellectually superior. (Bloom 1971, p. 18)

Social science emphasizes the need to conceptualize in part because of the need to remove some of these commonly held myths that Bloom refers to in the above quotation. Conceptualization is also important because if social scientists are to converse with each other then there needs to be some common and precise language available to them. Unfortunately social science has not achieved the extent of progress in the field of conceptualization that might have been expected. In the absence of a body of universally recognized and agreed definitions of central concepts, social scientists still feel it necessary to give their own definition of the concepts relating to their work.

The lack of agreement on the meaning of concepts is due in part to the fact that knowledge and events are constantly changing in the social world so that the task of identifying new concepts and redefining established ones is never finished. Indeed, a great deal of social science does not get much beyond this and as a result limits the efficiency of the next characteristic of social science: *the attempt at theorizing*. By this we mean the attempt to make statements of general validity about some particular phenomenon.

Theories are important in social science because they can lead to statements about society which can be researched and tested. If such statements (often referred to as hypotheses or propositions) are verified then this is seen as lending support to the theory from which they have been derived. On the other hand, if the hypotheses are found to be invalid then the theory itself is subject to criticisms which will lead to it being discarded, or altered, or to the hypotheses being further tested.

In the area of race relations, an interesting theory to explain the pattern of immigration is that the flow of immigrants into Britain was self-regulating in terms of demand for immigrant labour, but that this self-regulating flow was disrupted by the immigration control laws passed during the 1960s and 1970s. One hypothesis arising from this theory would be that immigration figures directly correlate with job vacancy figures. Insofar as this is true, then weight is given to the theory. If untrue then alternative hypotheses need to be explored before rejecting the theory itself. Research along these lines was in fact conducted by G. C. K. Peach and the results were published in 1968 in his book *West Indian Migration to Britain*. Peach showed that West Indian migration was very closely related to labour demand in the UK economy during the period 1955 to 1960 with migration increasing as labour demand increased and falling as demand for labour decreased. This pattern was disrupted from 1961 onwards due, Peach argued, to fear of immigration control which induced many to migrate who might not otherwise have done so.

This example illustrates what can be considered as rather narrow-range theorizing since it is limited to positing the relationship between a limited number of factors: in this case, immigration figures, demand for employment, and immigration controls. Theorizing can be much more wide-ranging than this and we shall be looking at some broad, all-encompassing theories later when we consider some of the alternative perspectives adopted by social scientists.

The final characteristic by which social science can be distinguished from everyday thinking concerns the way information is gathered, and especially the way in which investigation and inquiries to test hypotheses derived from theory are undertaken. This general area is referred to here as *methodological rigour* for short. By methodological rigour we mean that the social scientist takes special care with the validity and reliability of the methods and techniques used in studying human relationships. The following quotation expresses the concern that one social scientist felt about the methods he used for inquiring into a major pressure group that has operated in the field of race relations in Britain—the Campaign Against Racial Discrimination (CARD).

There is the methodological limitation inherent in pressure group studies stemming from the process of gathering information. A good deal of the material in this book comes from interviews, and the number of variables in informal, relatively unstructured interviewing are legion. A tape recorder was used to ensure accuracy of quotes, but the interpretative skills required in any historical reconstruction are especially challenged when there is a personal relationship (the interview) between the writer and those whom he presumes to write about, especially when that writer is both foreign and white. Basically, the interviews were an attempt to establish some of the undisputed facts about the organisation's history. They were also used to uncover what issues had concerned the particular interviewee—what her or his position had been, what was the basis of the conflict, what were the motives of the opposition, what was at stake? Obviously, I am also responsible for the reconstruction and the reader is invited to exercise his critical sense as he follows the story. (Heineman 1972, pp. xv–xvi)

The author in this extract discusses interviewing, which is a method frequently used by social scientists to gather information. Further consideration is given to this in chapter 3 in the content of social surveys. Heineman's book on CARD is also representative of another fundamental approach in social science, that of using case studies.

Method Box 1.2 Case Studies

Case studies in social science constitute detailed and intense descriptions of particular social, economic, political, or individual events or phenomena. They attempt to tell the story of how a particular event or phenomenon happened. Case studies exist, for example, on the many pressure groups that are involved in race relations, and on the background to the various public policies and Acts of Parliament in this area. Many other areas of social science have benefited from this method: case studies exist on the reorganization of secondary education, urban aid programmes, strikes, and innumerable other matters. They are very widely used especially in areas not previously studied and are valuable for stimulating insights and hypotheses to guide further research. The difficulties with case studies are that they tend to be overwhelmed with detail and their uniqueness means it is often impossible to draw generally valid conclusions from them.

In contrast to such social science techniques, and the care taken to ensure their validity and reliability, everyday thinking appears particularly deficient. We all tend to believe unreliable evidence given to us by 'someone who knows'. A notorious example of this was in the First World War when it was widely believed that Russian soldiers had landed in Britain 'with snow on their boots'. Or the story, attached to several towns in Napoleonic times which were said to have hanged a monkey in the belief, arising out of their ignorance of foreigners, that it was a French spy! Less dramatic—but equally unreliable—stories are believed every day. Similarly, in everyday life we tend to make generalizations about large groups from one or two examples or from anecdotal evidence drawn only from personal experience and which is likely to be unrepresentative of experience generally. 'I know someone who . . .' is not a valid basis for drawing conclusions in social science.

A good example of this from the earlier quotations representing everyday thinking on immigration is contained in the letter to the *Leicester Mercury*. The writer claims that most readers will agree with him. But how does he know? The social scientist would have to ask to see the evidence and critically examine the methods used to gather it. Similarly, Enoch Powell is quoted as claiming that whole

areas of the indigenous population have been dislodged. This allega-
tion was shown at the time to be totally false in the face of evidence
collected on the proportion of ethnic minorities in inner city electoral
wards. For the social scientist, then, a statement unsupported by
evidence collected with considerable care is no more than an asser-
tion and cannot be taken as a fact until shown to be so.

In the area of race relations the lack of methodological rigour in
everyday thinking leads to acceptance of stereotypes, which means
the practice of giving certain attributes to whole groups of people
despite the existence of factual evidence to the contrary. In this way,
for example, Jews are seen to be 'mean' and the Irish 'thick and
stupid'. A commonly held stereotype of 'the immigrant' is given in
one of the early quotations: 'illiterate, dirty and completely unsuited
and unused to our way of life.' Stereotypes exist on both sides as the
quotation from the West Indian person about 'white people' makes
plain: 'They are cursing you around the back.'

Concept Box 1.2 Stereotypes

A stereotype is an over-simplified mental picture of a person, group
of people, or an institution. The stereotype may refer to broad groups
such as blacks, Catholics, trade unions, or to narrow ones such as
Manchester United supporters, or dockers.

Stereotypes are usually accompanied by prejudice which is often,
though not always, unfavourable. Stereotypes are important
because they reinforce existing ways of thinking so that people see
only what they expect to see and their behaviour towards the stereotype is simplified. There is no need to decide what attitude or behaviour is appropriate because the stereotype makes this obvious. For
example, if someone believes that football supporters are drunken
hooligans then certain patterns of behaviour towards them will be
appropriate—ignore them, cross the road, and so on. If a football
supporter is lying down on the pavement, it is because he is drunk.
This stereotype will be reinforced by supporters who are drunk or
rowdy; evidence to the contrary will be ignored. Once formed,
stereotypes are difficult to change.

While critical of stereotypes that form the basis of some everyday
thinking, social scientists (and particularly social psychologists)
recognize that they are an essential way for people to process social
information in a complex world. It is the content of many everyday

stereotypes not the existence of stereotypes as such which is criticized by the social scientist.

Racial sterotypes found in everyday thinking derive from a variety
of sources all of which misrepresent reality. One of their sources is
the legacy of attitudes derived from slavery and Britain's imperial
past when the white man was seen as 'civilizing' the black man, who
was either portrayed as subhuman or patronizingly painted as 'the
noble savage'. These images live on and are fostered by statements
like the following one about certain Africans taken from a school
text book which until recently was to be found in many English
schools:

They have black skins. Their hair is curly and grows close to their heads.
Their lips are thick and red. When they dance they tap themselves and sing
queer sounds. They will dance or do anything for the white hunter because
they know he will give them tobacco and salt and perhaps arrows. (quoted in
Husband 1975, p. 84)

Stereotypes are also reflected in the mass media and thereby reinforced. It has been argued that the media present ethnic minorities as
both a threat and a problem and that this leads to feelings of hostility
towards such groups rather than acceptance of them.

Social Science Disciplines

So far we have been considering social science as a whole and analyz-
ing its major features as suggested in Method Box 1.1. However
'social science' is made up of several separate disciplines which share
these methodological features but which have individual characteristics and separate areas of study. It is possible to argue as to which
disciplines should be called 'social science' but for the purposes of
this chapter the following are highlighted: economics, politics,
sociology, social psychology, social policy and administration and
law. The different concerns and approaches of each of these disciplines will be illustrated by looking at various discipline-based books
on race relations. This strategy is preferred, at this stage, to the one
of presenting definitions of each discipline since these definitions
tend to be rather uninspiring and are usually highly contestable. The

first four of the disciplines to be covered here are also given considerable prominence in later chapters, so what follows is only an attempt to give an initial 'flavour' of their disinctive concerns.

Those who have some knowledge of *economics* might be forgiven for thinking that this discipline has nothing to offer to the study of race relations. But reference has already been made to one piece of economic research in this area, that by Peach into the relationship between immigration and job vacancies. Books on the economic dimensions of race relations have also been written. One of them, by Jones and Smith (1970), covers a variety of topics in which this discipline specializes. Chapters of their book deal with immigration and such topics as the immigrant population, their quantitative and qualitative impact on the labour force, their income and expenditure, their impact on social services in terms of public expenditure, their capital requirements, and their effect on economic growth, inflation, and the balance of payments.

The approach taken by the discipline of *politics* (alternatively called political studies, political science, or government) can be illustrated by Layton-Henry's *Politics of Race in Britain*. In the preface to his book he sets out his aim and in so doing demonstrates some of the concerns that his discipline has with race relations:

This book is an attempt to provide an accurate and up-to-date analysis of the politics of race in Britain. A detailed analysis of the processes and developments in Britain may help analysts and policy-makers in Europe and America to see the similarities and differences between their situation and the British case. A further reason for writing the book is that a considerable mythology has been created about many of the events and processes which are described here. The role of the major parties, of politicians and legislation has often been subject to varied and conflicting interpretations. The role of the 1948 Nationality Act, the controversies over the 1958 riots and the 1962 Commonwealth Immigrants Act are cases in point. Such controversies have continued and recently have surrounded the 1981 Nationality Act, the 1981 riots and the Scarman Report. In the recent general election of 1983 the importance of the black vote, the Conservatives appeal to black electors and the problem facing black candidates in gaining parliamentary nominations and securing election have all been the subject of heated debate. This book will attempt to explain clearly and accurately how the politics of race in Britain has reached its present state and what is likely to happen in the immediate future. The analysis will concentrate on the major developments and particularly on the role of the major political actors and institutions. (Layton-Henry 1984, pp. viii–ix)

Some of the terms used in the extract from Layton-Henry clearly distinguish it as a piece of writing by a political scientist; terms such as policy, parties, politicians, legislation, voting, elections, and parliament. Another term used by political scientists is that of pressure groups and a study of one of the pressure groups operating in the area of race relations was referred to earlier when the methodological approach taken by Heineman to his study of the Campaign Against Racial Discrimination was considered.

Sociology is the hardest discipline to describe. Cynics (usually from other social science disciplines) may claim that this is because it isn't really a discipline at all. One approach to defining sociology is to distinguish it from other disciplines on the grounds that it is concerned with what is left over in the social world from that which is claimed by other disciplines as economic, political, legal, psychological, or geographic. We could call this the reductionist view of sociology. Another approach sees sociology as synonymous with social science itself. Some introductory texts on social science turn out, for example, to be nothing more than introductions to the discipline of sociology. This could be called the imperialist view of sociology. The following quotation is representative of this imperialist view in that nearly all the social aspects of race relations are brought into focus in what purports to be a sociological study of race relations:

A number of vexed questions such as those of race and intelligence, arouse strong feelings among students of race relations. However, there are some other matters which fall more clearly into the area of sociological discussion which, though they may arouse less intense feelings, are considered at least intellectually problematic. Four of these lie at the very heart of the sociological study of race. The first is the question of whether the various elements of what we call 'racial problems'—prejudice, intolerance, discrimination and antagonism—can be explained largely in terms of a theory of domination or stratification. The second concerns the part played in race relations by *ideas* about race. The third concerns the part played by other psychological states associated with racial consciousness. And the fourth concerns the importance which sociologists should attach to the facts of *racial* differences as such. (Cohen 1976, p. 9)

The book from which this quotation comes is a compilation of articles and sections from other books (i.e. a reader). The first part of it is headed 'Sociological Perspectives' and has the following contents:

1 R. E. Park, Race and Culture.
2 Gunnar Myrdal, An American Dilemma.
3 S. N. Eisenstadt, The Absorption of Immigrants.
4 Oliver Cromwell Cox, Caste, Class, and Race.
5 Andrew Asherson, Race and Politics in South Africa.
6 Robert Blauner, Colonized and Immigrant Minorities.
7 R. A. Schermerhorn, Comparative Ethnic Relations.
8 Alfred Schutz, The Stranger.
9 John Rex, Race Relations and Sociological Theory.

The first, reductionist, interpretation of the content of sociology would stress its concern with the concepts such as those referred to in the titles above: *culture, stratification, consciousness, caste, class,* and *minorities.*

Social psychology is another difficult discipline to describe lying as it does between the parent disciplines of psychology and sociology. Thus social psychologists are never really too sure about their identity. In the area of race relations, for example, there are at least two social psychologies. One of these is what might be called the personality-and-prejudice approach with its emphasis on the origins of racially prejudiced attitudes in childhood and later life. The other social psychology emphasizes group processes whereby the evolution of prejudice is seen as a part of the formation and functioning of groups.

A reader on psychology and race relations edited by Watson and published in 1972 contained two parts. Part one was on aspects of interracial interaction and concentrated on racial awareness, prejudice, and self-identity. The second part of the reader was entitled 'The Race Variable and Key Issues in Social Psychology' and contained contributions from various authors on the following topics: culture, personality, and prejudice; family, marital, and child-bearing patterns in different ethnic groups; race and intelligence; alternatives to a personality-deficit interpretation of Negro under-achievement; sociolinguistics; psychiatric disorders in minority groups; crime and delinquency; and discrimination in personnel decisions.

While the four social science disciplines of economics, political science, sociology, and psychology are the major ones that are used in the rest of this book, it is necessary to acknowledge that there are others. Among them, two that have made a useful contribution to the study of race relations are now briefly introduced.

Social policy and administration is less well known. It has evolved largely in response to the development of the Welfare State and is mainly concerned with applying the concepts of the other social science disciplines to an understanding of the public and private provision of services like housing, health, education, income maintenance, and employment. The interest of this discipline in immigration and race relations can be seen from the following quotation:

New Commonwealth immigration to judge from the evidence available, was of three-fold significance for contemporary statutory social policy. To begin with, the mere presence of such newcomers in the country helped to show up some of the shortcomings—as well as some of the strengths—of Welfare State social services provision. Yet such a presence seemed, in the second place, to furnish not a passive commentary upon but an active test of the problem-solving capabilities of social service agencies faced by sometimes novel, sometimes controversial, and often greatly increased demands upon their facilities. Set against this, however, there was a third tendency apparent: for the social services themselves to feature as bones of contention in the host-immigrant context and for them thus to constitute a problem-exacerbating as well as a problem-solving resource. (Jones 1977, pp. 3–4)

Law can also claim to be a social science discipline and its interest in race relations is neatly contrasted with that of some other disciplines in the following extract from a book on legal control of racial discrimination:

Consequently much that a sociologist, social psychologist or economist would include in a work on this general subject is not to be found (herein): nothing is said about theories of racial stratification, of prejudice or of microeconomic models of discrimination. Conversely, much of the work devoted to matters that the black letter lawyer has defined out of his realm, as with the chapters on the condition of racial minorities in employment and the theoretical examination of concepts of discrimination. Thus the social reality of racial discrimination and disadvantage defines the setting of the study, a substantial proportion of which is devoted to highly detailed examination of the Race Relations Act 1976 ('the Act' or 'the 1976 Act') and related employment law. (Lustgarten 1980, p. ix)

As one might expect, law as a social science discipline is ultimately concerned with Acts of Parliament that affect race relations in all its aspects from employment to immigration control. But unlike practitioners of law—solicitors and lawyers—the discipline is also deeply concerned with the study of how law is made, how it is enforced, and with concepts like 'racial discrimination' which have taken on a special legal significance.

Having looked at the individual disciplines that make up social science, it is fitting to conclude with a rather lengthy quotation from one of the social scientists in Britain, Michael Banton, who has done much to develop an understanding of race relations. He argues in favour of an *interdisciplinary* approach to this field of study and in doing so provides further amplification on the character of the single-discipline approach and the characteristics of social science that were identified earlier. As an example of a piece of social science writing, it is clearly different from the examples of everyday thinking with which this chapter began.

For a variety of reasons it is unlikely that the study of race relations will ever occupy a place in the map of learning similar to those held by physics, economics, and French literature. But there are other fields of research and teaching, such as engineering, criminology, commerce, international relations, social administration, and public health, which also bring together knowledge gained within other disciplines. The difference between these two kinds of 'subject' is sometimes expressed as the difference between pure and applied sciences. A pure science, such as physics or economics, concentrates upon distinctive theoretical problems. An applied science, such as engineering, draws upon work in the pure sciences (as, in this case, physics, chemistry, mathematics, etc.) for the elucidation of particular problems which tend to be of a less abstract character. In this light the study of race relations may be viewed as an applied social science. It brings together all that other sciences can contribute to the solution of problems within its own special field. It draws not only on the pure social sciences, such as psychology, economics, political science, and sociology, but upon the perspective and expertise which historians and geographers can furnish for the better understanding of relations in particular regions. As with other applied social sciences, how a particular course is taught in a particular university may be influenced by the discipline in which the teacher has received most of his training, but this is not necessarily a disadvantage, since a certain bias towards a particular discipline may give a teaching course greater coherence.

The student of psychology, economics, political science, or sociology is not interested in race relations as such, but in questions of human behaviour. Studying a complex situation, the pure social scientist will concentrate his attention upon just a few variables in it which he will try to relate to similar phenomena in other situations. His task is one of analysis. At other times, however, both social scientists and general readers need a synoptic interpretation of the position . . . On the one hand, the accumulation of theoretical and descriptive material in this field during the past two generations

is now so extensive and interrelated that it can be used as a basis for impart-
ing intellectual discipline and for training students in the marshalling of data
and argument. On the other hand, the progressive specialization of the pure
social sciences increases the significance of subjects which bring together
modes of analysis used by other departments of study. One weakness of
specialized training is that students become wedded to particular theories
and approaches, regarding them as better than others, so that they are
unable to appreciate the limits within which these ideas are useful. Thus an
applied social science provides a measure of synthesis which is an essential
balance to the analytical propensities of the pure sciences. (Banton 1967,
pp. 2-3)

In advocating an interdisciplinary approach to race relations
Banton begins by arguing in this extract that race relations is an
'applied' rather than a 'pure' area of study. By this he means that
academic interest in race relations should be directed more to
attempting to solve problems posed by it than to armchair theorizing. An example to illustrate the difference between 'applied' and
'pure' academic study from the physical sciences would be between
building a bridge (a practical problem) and the calculation of metal
stresses (a theoretical issue). Banton's other main point is that the
problems posed by race relations (note we have avoided saying
'caused by') can only be solved by pooling the specialized knowledge
that has been developed to date by the separate disciplines working
largely in isolation from each other. Clearly political, economic,
social, geographic, and psychological aspects of race relations are
interrelated. Thus if social science is to offer any real enlightenment
in this area and in particular to offer solutions to the problems raised
by it, then a synthesis of all these aspects needs to be developed.

In the chapters that follow the contribution that different social
science disciplines can make to an understanding of the chosen
dimensions of people's lives are considered. The final chapters will
return to the problem of relating these disciplinary insights together.

Contrasting Perspectives

In the major part of this chapter we have presented some of the common ingredients of social science in terms of the methodological
characteristics that it possesses and which contrast in many ways
with everyday thinking. As we have seen from our brief look at the
social science disciplines, social science is not a cohesive and unified
body of study. A truly interdisciplinary social science is still very

much a hope rather than a fact. In addition to the different disciplines, there is another source of difference within social science, that
of the contrasting perspectives which guide and influence the work
of individual social scientists and which cross the disciplinary
boundaries. These perspectives represent the different ways by
which social scientists conceive of society and interpret evidence
about it. They are broad, all-encompassing theories which reflect in
part the values of their adherents. We shall consider four of the perspectives: those of individualism, pluralism, élitism, and Marxism.
There are others that we could have chosen but these seem to be the
most important at the present time.

Each of these perspectives on society is enormously complex and
all that can be offered here is a general introduction to them. To help
in this, the diagrams in Figure 1.1 present the perspectives in their
simplest form.

The various perspectives that can be found within social science
can be explained rather more fully by looking at their alternative

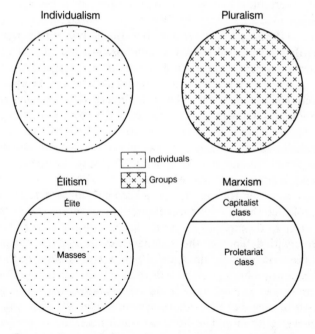

Fig. 1.1   Contrasting Perspectives on the Structure of Society

views about four different aspects of society. The chosen aspects of society relate to the political dimension of society because it is this dimension that most clearly demonstrates the essential differences between them. Later, the differences between the perspectives will be further highlighted by a consideration of how each perspective would begin to understand, select, and interpret evidence, and theorize about race relations.

The four aspects of society that are used to explain the contrasting perspectives arise from a consideration of the following questions:

(1) What is the basic unit for analysing society?
(2) What is the role of the state in society?
(3) What is the basis for the authority exercised by those in political control?
(4) What are the major priorities in the making of public policy?

Of the four perspectives examined, the individualist perspective comes closest to what we have referred to earlier as everyday thinking. As a social science perspective it was particularly prevalent in the nineteenth century but has re-emerged in recent years and closely corresponds to what is now termed the New Right ideas which are associated with the Thatcherite wing of the Conservative Party. As the diagram above indicates, the individualist perspective primarily conceives of society as composed of individuals and the assumption here is that these individuals are rational and capable of knowing their own best interest. Individuals which make up society are also seen as largely shaped by their inherited biological make-up and minimal acknowledgement is given to the way in which the social structure influences the values and interests of people. The biological make-up of individuals is seen as relatively fixed and summed up in the phrase 'human nature' which itself is often conceived of in a negative way as something which needs to be controlled. Hence a primary role seen for the state is to keep law and order. The other main role that the individualist perspective sees for the state is that of protection of the country from external aggression. Law and order, together with defence, as the essential roles of the state are summed up in the term 'laissez-faire state' which is used to describe the situation in Britain in the first part of the nineteenth century. Political activity is seen as consisting of individuals pursuing their own self-interests by means of the electoral system and individual action. This political activity should be directed to ensuring freedom for the individual. As a bulwark for this freedom, the preservation of private property and the untrammelled operation of the free market economy are seen to be essential, as well as making for an efficient use of resources.

The pluralist perspective developed from an awareness of the increasing importance of groups as opposed to individuals as the basic unit of society. Groups in this sense are taken to refer to organizations which seek to advance the interests or values of their members. They include not only trade unions and bodies like the Institute of Directors, but also the Church of England, Greenpeace, the Campaign for Nuclear Disarmament, and the Scouts. They also include less clearly organized groups like families and ethnic groups. Industrial societies are seen as marked by a great number and complexity of such groups. They are related to each other by virtue of the fact that membership of them overlaps and cross-cutting ties are therefore made between them. Although the political system is seen as responding to the demands of all of these groups, two kinds of groups emerge as of particular importance politically. These political groups are first political parties and second pressure groups. The distinction between them is that pressure groups are content to influence public policies, while parties wish to gain the reins of government itself.

The role of the state in the pluralist perspective is considered to be a neutral one in the sense that the state is not seen as having any self-interest of its own but merely acts to implement those demands which groups agree on as a result of bargaining and competition between them. Groups are seen to compete on a relatively equal basis with the influence of one group being countervailed by that of another. The authority of the state rests on its effectiveness in implementing these demands and facilitating the process of achieving consensus (agreement on policy). Such consensus is expected to improve equality of opportunity for such benefits as education, to provide public welfare services, and to restrain the worst excesses of the market economy.

More recently the pluralist perspective has been refined to what is sometimes referred to as neo-pluralism. Neo-pluralism incorporates evidence of the independent influence of government and the increasingly positive role that it plays in the affairs of society beyond that of acting as the arbiter between competing groups. Neo-pluralism also considers that many of the more significant groups—especially parties and pressure groups—appear to be controlled by the few who lead them rather than all the members who are associated with them. Group competition is thus seen as limited to competition between the leaders of groups who may not always represent the best interests of their members. In other respects, neo-pluralism does not depart too far from the original perspective.

The third perspective of élitism stands in sharp contrast to that of pluralism. From the élitist perspective, all societies, whatever their stage of development, political persuasion, or economic organiza-tion, like all groups within society, can be divided into an élite who control and the masses who are led. Élites may be formed from a variety of alternative bases—religion, bureaucracy, hereditary privilege, control of information—and the state comes under their control. The mass of the people, on the other hand, is seen as composed of isolated, often alienated, individuals who have little or no control over the élite. Indeed, in many élitist theories the masses are seen as psychologically predisposed to be led and deferential to those who control them. The policies pursued by the state depend upon the interests and beliefs of the élite who happen to be in control.

The élitist perspective has been developed in part as a counter-perspective to that of Marxism. In talking of a Marxist perspective we need to distinguish Marxism as a way of understanding society from Marxism as a body of ideas (ideology) about how society should be changed. From a Marxist perspective the basic unit for analysing society is economic class. Class is also recognized as important in the pluralist perspective which sees the different classes as groups made up of those with similar market situations with regard to possessions, property, and job opportunities. In the Marx-ist perspective, however, class is seen as being determined by the nature and organization of the economic processes of production. Thus in a society dominated by a capitalist, free market mode of pro-duction, the two significant classes from a Marxist perspective are the capitalist (or bourgeoisie) who own and control the means of production such as factories, and the proletariat (or workers) who lack that ownership and control.

The state in the Marxist perspective is considered to be the instru-ment of the capitalist class. As Marx put it, the state is a committee for managing the common affairs of the whole bourgeoisie. The relationship between the two economic classes is seen as one of fun-damental conflict. This conflict, however, is reduced by numerous mechanisms which seek to limit the extent to which the proletariat is conscious of its separate interests and potential power. In the political sphere the institutions associated with liberal democracy like elections and parliaments are viewed as fundamentally methods for disguising and legitimizing the capitalists' control of the state. The state is used to maintain the capitalist system and central to this is the need to sustain the profitability of private companies and to limit the power of organized labour.

As with pluralism, the Marxist perspective is subject to changes and these have been summed up by the phrase structural Marxism. The more contemporary formulation of the Marxist perspective departs from the above description in a few major respects. Structural Marxism, for example, recognizes a more independent role for the state and in particular the bureaucracy of full-time officials of which it is largely composed. There is also an increasing acknowledgement of divisions within the capitalist class such as that between financiers and industrialists. The contemporary structural Marxist perspective also acknowledges more fully the importance of other divisions in society and especially those of gender and race.

The four perspectives that have been outlined are a useful way of comparing and contrasting the work of different social scientists. We need to take into consideration the influence of these underlying perspectives in the accounts social scientists give of social phenomena. This applies particularly to an area such as race relations. The perspective held by any one social scientist will influence which dimensions of this aspect of society is chosen for consideration, which more narrow-range theories and evidence are put forward, and what actions are recommended. This can best be illustrated by taking as an example the inner-city 'riots' in ethnically diverse areas.

In considering such riots there would only be a limited amount of agreement between social scientists representing the different perspectives. Such agreement might be limited to acknowledging the existence of certain obvious facts: shops were set alight and goods stolen; stones and missiles were thrown at the police; the police used charges and tear-gas to disperse those involved. But in the selection of further facts, descriptions of what took place, and especially interpretations of what happened and why it happened, considerable disagreements would soon emerge. These disagreements might well follow the outlines of the perspectives we have considered.

From an individualist perspective the inner-city riots might be seen as solely due to criminal activity by a group of individual vandals lacking the necessary parental upbringing and intelligence to curb their natural aggressive instincts. Such indiscipline and lack of intelligence might even be associated with the supposed racial characteristics of those involved. The solution from this perspective would be to strengthen the hand of the police to maintain law and order. There might well be calls for repatriation from those who stress the racial dimension. The idea that those involved are the victims of social deprivation would be dismissed as woolly-minded.

A pluralist explanation would be very different. It would begin by looking at the group dynamics of the situation, at the cultural norms among deprived inner-city groups, at their lack of access to more acceptable ways of influencing affairs, and bring into play other more hidden facts in the situation like that of unemployment. The Scarman report of 1981 into the Brixton disorders appears to have adopted the pluralist position and this is what it had to say about black unemployment:

The reasons for the higher level of unemployment among young black people are, no doubt, many and various. Lack of qualifications, difficulties arising from unrealistic expectations, bad time-keeping, unwillingness to travel and, most important of all, trouble with the English language are factors which, it has been suggested to me, play a part. It seems clear, however, that discrimination—by employers and at the work place—is a factor of considerable importance, and one for which the sustained efforts of the local authority, the Careers Service and the Manpower Services Commission to place young people in work cannot easily compensate. Much of the evidence of discrimination is indirect rather than direct: but I have no doubt that it is a reality which all too often confronts the black youths of Brixton. (Scarman Report 1981, pp. 10–11)

To the pluralist, the solution is to strengthen the involvement of disadvantaged groups by developing community forums and liaison committees between inner-city residents, the police, and their local authorities. The more contemporary pluralists—the neo-pluralists—would also argue for more government intervention to reduce unemployment, to increase resources available for inner-city development, and for public action against discrimination.

From the élitist perspective the riots would be seen as the alienated response of a section of the mass of the people—unorganized, spontaneous, and powerless. The police would be seen as enforcing control over the masses in support of the prevailing élite. The lack of access of black people to that élite would be emphasized. Nothing could be changed except that the experience of the force by which the élite can react would tend to quell further rioting, at least for the short term.

The social scientist from a Marxist perspective would interpret the riots in yet another way. The rioters would be seen in class terms as a section of the working class; the police would be seen as state agents acting on behalf of the bourgeousie to maintain the capitalist system. The existence of the riots would be taken as an indication of the inherent conflict between these classes in a capitalist society and perhaps evidence of capitalism in crisis. That many of the rioters were black would be seen as due to their precarious situation under capitalism where they make up a reserve army of labour which is dispensable at times of recession. This latter idea is reflected in the following quotation about black unemployment which clearly contrasts with the pluralist interpretation in the Scarman Report:

Black . . . make up the most easily expendable parts of the workforce. They are today's equivalent of what Marx referred to in the nineteenth century as 'the reserve army of labour'—i.e. that section of the population which can be sucked into employment when the economy is expanding (thus helping to keep wages down by increasing the supply of labour as demand increases) and which can be pushed out again when it collapses back into recession. Where . . . blacks have managed to resist this and to hang on to their jobs, they have become easy scapegoats to be offered up to white male workers who are all too often ready to accept that unemployment is caused by increased numbers of blacks . . . in the labour force. Where they have failed to resist it, they may still be scapegoated as 'scroungers' living off social security while white workers pay taxes to support them. Either way, their employment situation is unenviable. (Dearlove & Saunders 1984, p. 191)

What makes this a Marxist interpretation, as well as the reference to Marx himself, is the emphasis that is given to the economy, and especially the needs of capitalism, as the determinant of black unemployment. It also emphasizes how race conflict exists to divide and mislead the working class. From this perspective a 'solution' to inner-city riots requires a fundamental alteration in the structural factors that give rise to it and that essentially means that nothing can really be done until capitalism is overthrown.

Each perspective, then, offers a very different understanding of the same phenomenon, in this case inner-city riots, and each comes to very different conclusions about it. In the final analysis it is impossible to advise the reader objectively which perspective he or she should adopt. In its own way, each offers a more or less satisfactory understanding of society. And such perspectives are needed because 'facts' do not speak for themselves. Facts have to be selected and interpreted. What is important is to recognize that the contrasting perspectives exist and to be able to take into account the influence that they have on accounts drawn from them. Your understanding of society will be coloured by your prejudices and beliefs whether you recognize it or not. And these may approximate to one or other of these perspectives. In everyday thinking, however, the perspectives are not used consistently and are not at a very high level of understanding. The fundamental task of those wishing to depart from everyday thinking about society and to enter the realm of social science is first of all to become aware of their personal perspective and then to be willing rationally to consider the value of alternative perspectives.

References

Banton, M. (1967). *Race Relations*. London: Tavistock.

Bloom, L. (1971). *The Social Psychology of Race Relations*. London: Allen & Unwin.

Cohen, P. (1976). 'Race Relations as a Sociological Issue'. In G. Bowker and J. Carner (1976). *Race and Ethnic Relations*. London: Hutchinson.

Dearlove, J., and P. Saunders (1984). *Introduction to British Politics*. Cambridge: Polity.

Duverger, M. (1964). *Introduction to the Social Sciences*. London: Allen & Unwin.

Finnigan, R. (1976). *Inquiry in the Social Sciences*. Open University Course U202, Unit 20. Milton Keynes: Open University Press.

Hallett, G. (1974). 'The Political Economy of Immigration Control'. In C. Wilson *et al.* (1974). *Economic Issues in Immigration*. London: Institute of Economic Affairs.

Heineman, B. (1972). *The Politics of the Powerless*. Oxford: OUP.

Husband, C. (1974). *Racism and the Mass Media*. London: Davis-Poynter.

———(ed.) (1975). *White Media and Black Britain*. London: Arrow Books.

———(ed.) (1982). *Race Relations*. London: Hutchinson.

Jones, C. (1977). *Immigration and Social Policy in Britain*. London: Tavistock.

Jones, K., and A. D. Smith (1970). *The Economic Impact of Commonwealth Immigration*. London: Cambridge University Press.

Lustgarten, L. (1980). *Legal Control of Racial Discrimination*. London: Macmillan.

Layton-Henry, Z. (1984). *Politics of Race in Britain*. London: Allen & Unwin.

Mitchell, G. D. (1968). *A Dictionary of Sociology*. London: Routledge & Kegan Paul.

Peach, G. C. K. (1968). *West Indian Migration to Britain*. Oxford: OUP.

Rose, E. J. B. *et al*. (1969). *Colour and Citizenship*. Oxford: OUP.

Scarman Report. (1981). *The Brixton Disorders 10–12 April 1981*. London: HMSO, Cmnd 8427.

Smithies, B., and P. Fiddick (1969). *Enoch Powell on Immigration*. London: Sphere.

Troyna, B. (1981). *Public Awareness and the Media*. London: Commission for Racial Equality.

Watson, P. (ed.) (1972). *Psychology and Race*. Harmondsworth: Penguin.

Young, K., and P. Connelly (1981). *Policy and Practice in the Multi-Racial City*. London: PSI.

2 People, Work, and Unemployment

Work is like love. Those without it want it, whilst some of those with it wish it would go away. Work dominates some people's lives and the hours they spend working reflects this primacy. For others work is a necessary evil, something that has to be done in order to make possible more important things in life. For another group, obtaining work is about as likely as winning the pools; it is possible but it isn't likely.

The dominating effect of work on life and language is evident in my thesaurus which lists over a hundred synonyms for it. These range from *drudgery*, *effort*, and *grind*, through *profession*, *achievement*, and *creation*, to *manipulate* and *exploit*. This range of synonyms illustrates the diversity of the influence of work on life. Its importance is not just that it takes up so many hours and directly affects living standards, but that work—and its absence—affects the way that people think and act in areas of life which seem to be far removed from the world of work.

Given its importance in our lives, it is not surprising that social scientists from many disciplines have studied various aspects of work and Figure 2.1 illustrates the areas of interest related to work of four social science disciplines. The Figure over-simplifies in a number of ways. In the first place there is a good deal of overlap between some disciplines so that social psychologists, for example, make use of two disciplines. Moreover people from differing disciplines often study the same topic so that trade unions, for example, would be of interest to people from very different academic backgrounds. Another complication arises because work links up with other areas, so that a sociologist interested in the role of women would look at work, not for its own sake, but because work—and the lack of it—has a large impact on the whole life-style of women. Thus the diagram is not meant to give a complete picture, but merely to illustrate some of the very varied concerns of social scientists from various disciplines in the area.

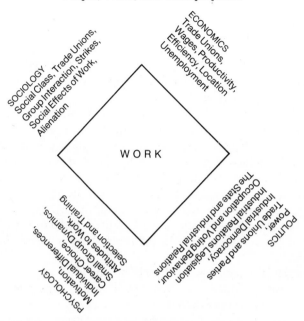

Fig. 2.1 Disciplinary Approaches to the Study of Work

This chapter does not attempt to cover work in all its aspects. That would require a large team of social scientists and several volumes. Instead we pick and choose. We start by asking why people work. This leads to a discussion on the influences of work on people's lives. We then reverse the view and consider unemployment, its effects, and one theory which suggests a way for governments to tackle the problem.

This line of approach has been chosen not only because it focuses on several areas of interest to different disciplines, but also because it allows us to examine a number of methods and problems which are relevant to other topics in social science. Thus by studying work and unemployment we develop social science skills which are applicable in other areas.

Why Work?

The answer to the question 'Why work?' might seem obvious. We work because we have to in order to obtain money in order to buy the things we need. There is a good deal of truth in that response. For most of human history most people have been forced to work in order to eat.

However, in recent decades, in the most advanced countries in the world, the position has become more complex. In part this change has occurred because of changes in what is meant by 'work'. In medieval times relatively little work was done for money. People worked at home or in the fields looking after animals or crops and received—some—of the produce. With the industrial revolution came an increasing division of labour so that some people stayed at home whilst others went out to work for pay in shops, offices, or factories. The word 'work' is now usually reserved for this kind of activity. In advanced economies less than half the population go out to work in this sense. 'Non-workers' include not only the idle and the rich, but also housewives, children, the retired, and the unemployed. Many of these 'non-workers' actually work much harder than the 'workers'!

However, the main reason why it is too simple to argue that people go out to work in order to eat is not because of changing definitions of work. Few workers would starve if they ceased to go to work, but they continue to do so. This can be seen most clearly if we consider those who work despite being wealthy enough not to need to work, or those such as pensioners with a guaranteed income who still choose to work.

People work for more than money. One reason for this is the satisfaction which some people obtain from their work. This is not only true for people with exciting or interesting jobs—TV reporters, surgeons, actors—but it also applies to many whose work is much more mundane. This is most apparent in the caring professions such as teaching and nursing, but it also applies to those whose work offers an opportunity to employ skills as diverse as those of the carpenter or steelworker. Where people obtain satisfaction from their work they may be willing to work even though they could manage without the money it brings them. An opinion poll in Britain carried out a survey of employed people and asked 'Do you enjoy the work you do a lot, a little, or not at all?' Seventy-five per cent answered, 'A lot.' The same survey found that a majority would not give up work even if they could do so without loss of income (Jahoda 1979, p. 493). This is not to deny, of couse, that many people dislike their work and would be delighted to give it up if their income made this possible.

Socialization

Money and satisfaction are not the only reasons why people work. A much less obvious reason is that we are socialized into thinking that we ought to work.

Concept Box 2.1 Socialization

Socialization is one of the most important concepts in social science, with an application much wider than the world of work. It has been defined as:

The process whereby the individual is moulded into a social being through learning to think and behave according to the values and norms prevalent in his society. It is how a person becomes part of a society. (Thomlinson 1965, pp. 9–10)

So socialization is the process by which individuals adapt to their environment by interacting with other people. We learn what kind of behaviour is appropriate in different circumstances—it is all right to sing in the bath but not at a meeting. Socialization is a lifelong process, but it is particularly important in childhood, for it is as a child that the individual is most malleable and adaptable. The family is particularly important in this process; that is why most children follow the belief systems—such as religion—of their parents. The specific processes by which socialization takes place are not fully understood, though some are obvious, such as *imitation*; for example when a child copies its mother in some activity. Another way in which socialization takes place is by *identification*; for example a child may identify with its friends and take on not only their mannerisms and ways of dressing but also their attitudes and beliefs.

Social scientists try to understand and explain the world about them. One problem of crucial importance is to explain how societies hang together—or to put it negatively—why societies don't keep breaking up? One answer to this question is that most people tend to have similar values and beliefs to those around them, so that beliefs about how a country should be run tend to change very slowly. A child born in Saudi Arabia, will probably become a Muslim, one born in Moscow a communist. These are specific examples of the general rule that the inhabitants of any country tend to adopt—often unconsciously—the predominant belief systems of that country. This belief ranges from the trivial, such as the 'correct' way to use a knife and fork, to the significant, like the way in which a country should be run. There are a number of ways in which social scientists explain this phenomenon, but perhaps the most convincing explanations make use of the concept of socialization.

Socialization is concerned not only with attitudes and beliefs, but also with behaviour. We learn whilst still young that it is wrong to steal, that we should not hit other people, that boys should not cry, that we should obey the law and those in authority such as teachers. The process is not always successful. In many cases socialization is incomplete and people break the law, ignore teachers, and eat peas with a spoon, but the socialization process is successful enough so that most of us not only know how we ought to behave but feel guilty when we do not behave correctly.

Socialization continues into adult life, and one way in which adult socialization takes place is through experience at work. People joining a firm are usually very quick to adopt the attitudes and practices of their workmates.

On a larger scale, the inhabitants of a country learn the attitudes towards work of that society. These attitudes are not necessarily spread deliberately, but they permeate the mass media, the educational system, and even religion. Thus, a Church of England bishop in 1786 wrote that in Sunday School children were enjoined 'under pain of eternal punishment, and with the promise of eternal rewards, the great duties of sobriety, industry, veracity, honesty, humility, patience, content, resignation to the will of God, and submission to the authority of their superiors . . .' (Booth 1980, p. 115). One of the most influential sociologists, Max Weber, analysed the relationship between religion and capitalism in a book called *The Protestant Ethic and the Spirit of Capitalism*.

Profile 2.1 Max Weber (1864–1920)

His Life

Max Weber was born in Erfurt in what was then Prussia on 21 April

1864, though the family soon moved to Berlin. His family background was Prussian middle-class Protestantism. His father was a lawyer and civil servant who provided an intellectual background which stimulated the young Weber's development. His father was domineering, his mother very devout, and his parents lived together in a kind of institutionalized estrangement.

Weber's secondary education concentrated on languages, history, and the classics and he then attended three German universities, concentrating on law. He also spent a lot of time on student activities, such as drinking, carousing, and duelling. In 1891 he qualified as a university teacher and in the following year married his second cousin and obtained a minor position teaching law and later economics.

In 1898 he quarrelled with his father who died before the quarrel could be resolved. Weber suffered a nervous breakdown and it was almost twenty years before he again took up a university teaching post. In the mean time he travelled and wrote a number of books and articles. In the First World War he worked as a hospital administrator.

After the War he continued the life of a private scholar but attempted to enter politics as a candidate for the German Democratic Party but was not selected as a candidate. He obtained a post as Professor of Sociology but died shortly afterwards in 1920 at the age of 56.

His ideas

Weber's life and work were filled with contradictions. He was a nationalist who criticized his country, an analyst of power politics who failed even to be selected as a party candidate, a monarchist who denounced the Kaiser, and later an individualist who believed in strong party leadership.

Weber engaged in a lifelong argument with Marxism. The essence of Weber's position was that individual action should be the unit of sociological analysis and that social science should attempt to be value-free in the sense that the investigator should keep his own values and beliefs separated from the areas he was researching.

He developed his analysis of the Protestant Ethic into an analysis of contemporary religion including a study of Confucianism and Hinduism, pointing out that whilst material factors are important, ideas can also be crucial determinants of social change.

Weber also developed the notion of 'ideal types'. By 'ideal' he did not mean that they were good or should be sought after, but that the type contained the quintessential features to a degree that would not be found in real life. In other words 'ideal' means a kind of abstract model. He analysed three ideal types of authority: charismatic, traditional, and legal. Charismatic authority rests on extraordinary personal qualities which inspire followers—characters as diverse as Napoleon and Ghandi possessed this type of authority. Traditional authority rests on customs and practices deriving from the past: the leader must be obeyed because this is the way things have always been done. Legal-rational authority rests on the appeal to formally laid-down rules and laws such as are found in bureaucracy. The leader should be obeyed because he is properly appointed and rules within the law.

Weber had a particular interest in bureaucracy which he believed was the characteristic type of social organization in Western capitalist societies. In a bureaucracy business is conducted in accordance with laid-down rules and procedures, work is carried out on the basis of impersonal criteria, authority is delegated where necessary. The bureaucrat is appointed on the basis of qualifications, exercises authority impersonally and is rewarded by a career which provides a salary and the possibility of advancement. Bureaucracy is a suitable form of social organization for an industrial country because of its precision, continuity, and uniformity of operation. Weber believed that the increasing demands of society for more order and regulation, and the increasing extent of the division of labour, would tend to produce more and more bureaucratization.

His importance

It is hard to evaluate the importance of a social scientist of such stature. Many of his ideas have become widely accepted, if sometimes in a dis-torted form. The notion of 'charismatic personalities' derives from his work and so does the idea of a work ethic, sometimes applied even to non-Christian societies such as Japan.

A more accurate impression of his influence can be obtained by glan-cing through any textbook of sociology where his ideas will influence much of the content. That is not to suggest that his ideas are always accepted, for all Weber's ideas have been subject to criticism.

His ideas permeate social science. The International Encyclopaedia of Social Science gives under his biography cross references to the areas where his influence is important. These are: Administration, Alienation, Authority, Buddhism, Bureaucracy, Caste, Charisma, Chinese Society, Christianity, City, Creativity . . .

The Protestant Work Ethic

Weber suggested that people adopt ideas to fit in with their interests and showed that Puritanism, although its primary interest was service to God, also helped to create the conditions which were needed if capitalism were to develop. The Puritan doctrine of predestination suggested that one's salvation or damnation was determined by God, and that there should be no priesthood to mediate between man and God. True faith—and an indication of future salvation—showed itself in a way of life which gave glory to God and manifested itself by worldly success. To achieve success needed individual responsibility, hard work, thrift, the application of reason rather than sentiment to business, and the reinvestment of profits. An individual's position in life was his own responsibility. These qualities necessary for business success were those which were emphasized by the Protestant view of religion and meant that Protestants tended to become the leaders of capitalism. As Weber noted:

A glance at the occupational leaders of a country of mixed religious composition brings to light the remarkable frequency a situation which has several times provoked discussion in the Catholic press and literature, and in Catholic congresses in Germany, namely, the fact that business leaders and owners of capital, as well as the higher grades of skilled labour, and even more the higher technically and commercially trained personnel of modern enterprises, are overwhelmingly Protestant (Weber 1930, p. 35)

This attitude towards business spread from Protestants to permeate whole societies. It meant that the attitude towards work which Weber called 'traditionalism'—being unwilling to work harder than was needed to earn the necessities of life—became reprehensible. To work was good: to work hard was better. Those who did not work, unless they had some reason such as severe illness or care of young children, were considered idle layabouts, spongers on society.

Concept Box 2.2 Capitalism

A dictionary of social science defines capitalism as 'an economic system in which the greater proportion of economic life, particularly ownership of and investment in production goods, is carried on under private (i.e. non-governmental) auspices through the process of economic competition and the avowed incentive of profit' (Gould and Kolb 1964, p. 70).

The two main characteristics of capitalism are therefore private ownership of the means of production and distribution (e.g. factories, offices, and shops) together with an emphasis on the profit motive as an incentive to economic action. From a Marxist perspective a third feature of capitalism is that the owners of the means of production exploit the workers.

In practice capitalism is a somewhat vague term which is used to describe a wide variety of societies, but the main difference between capitalist and socialist is that the former are dominated by private property and production whilst socialist societies emphasize state ownership.

The extent to which the Protestant work ethic prevails today is a matter for argument, and clearly the work ethic has been rejected by many groups in society. Nevertheless for many people work is undertaken not only for money, or the satisfaction it brings, but because it is felt right and proper that able-bodied people should work. A person without a job may well lose not only the respect of others, but his own self-respect. People work because they have been socialized into accepting without question the value of society that work is a virtue.

The Effects of Work

Income

One consequence of work is that it affects the distribution of income within a country. It does not *determine* the distribution of incomes, for many people receive incomes that do not derive from work. The most obvious example is income arising from investments. This has a particularly important effect on the distribution of income, for the better-off sections of the community may well derive a large part of their income from investment rather than work. At the opposite end of the income scale, many of the poorest in the community also receive income from non-work sources, though in this case the income is often in the form of pensions or social security benefits.

Method Box 2.1 The Problem of Definition and Measurement

In everyday life there is usually no need to make exact statements. 'It's a large house' or 'There were a lot of people at the funeral' are quite precise enough to convey the information required by the listener.

However, in social science considerable precision is needed. It is not clear exactly what is meant if we say that a country is 'poor', that certain people are 'politically active', or that 'houses are over-crowded'. Such terms need to be defined precisely in order to make analysis possible.

That is only half the story. Measurement is an important technique in social science, but accurate measurement of social variables is almost always difficult. There is no ruler available to measure atti-tudes, no scale to weigh educational achievement. Thus researchers often have to invent measures—for example by constructing ques-tionnaires to measure attitudes. Another device is to use proxies, for example to use examination results in a few subjects as a measure of total educational achievement which cannot be measured directly. Even where statistics are available—for example of the number of houses—it may not be possible to say how many of them are in a 'satisfactory' condition. As these examples show, it is often easier to measure quantity rather than quality.

Whilst social scientists from different disciplinary backgrounds are interested in the distribution of income, it is of particular concern to economists. Their work in this area illustrates many of the diffi-culties facing social scientists studying other aspects of social science. These difficulties can most conveniently be summarized under two headings: conceptual difficulties such as deciding pre-cisely what is meant by 'income', and practical difficulties arising from the inadequacy of data.

Conceptual difficulties

Before it is possible to measure incomes, it is necessary to decide precisely what should be included. This is not as easy as it sounds. Which of the following should be counted as 'income'?

(a) vegetables grown in my garden and sold to neighbours;
(b) vegetables grown in my garden and eaten by me;
(c) a legacy or gift from a friend or relative;
(d) income received from selling shares;
(e) shares rising in price and making me richer even though I don't sell them;
(f) someone repaying a debt owed to me;
(g) payments by my employer to a pension fund from which I will ultimately benefit.

There is no 'correct' answer to these questions, and in practice answers vary between researchers and between countries. Most economists would accept a definition such as 'income in a given period is the amount a person could have spent while maintaining the value of his/her wealth intact.' Using this definition (a), (b), (c), and (e) should be counted as income, and probably (g) as well, though this would depend on the precise rights the employee had over money in the pension fund.

Even if there were some clear and unambiguous way to decide what was meant by income, other problems arise. Should income be counted before or after tax? Should we be concerned with incomes received by individuals or by the family—and if the latter what exactly do we mean by 'family'?

Practical difficulties

It is only rarely that social scientists can obtain precisely the data they would like. Shortage of accurate data is a very real problem to those investigating the distribution of income. The major difficulty is that people are unwilling to disclose their incomes unless compelled to do so by law. Some countries obtain details of incomes from census type surveys, but the usual source is the income tax returns submitted to the tax authorities. This has two consequences: the question 'What is income?' discussed under conceptual difficulties is in practice answered by 'income is whatever the tax authorities say is income.' The other consequence is that the statistics obtained are inaccurate because people have strong incentives to reduce their actual incomes in their tax declarations.

Cross-country comparisons are difficult because different authorities define income differently and because they collect the statistics in different ways. Nevertheless some comparisons can be made,

Table 2.1. Distribution of Taxable Incomes of Families

Income share of the

Country	Top 1%	Top 5%	Top 20%	21–80%	81–100%
UK	6	16	39	53	8
FRG	4	14	39	57	4
USA	8	21	48	49	3
Ireland	5	15	39	52	7

Source: Derived from the *Royal Commission on the Distribution of Income and Wealth* Report No. 5 Cmnd. 7595 HMSO London (1977).

though with caution. For example, the figures in Table 2.1 for the USA are not strictly comparable with the others because husbands and wives often submit separate returns and so are treated as separate families. Another complication is that the Irish data are restricted to non-agricultural incomes.

In a state of complete equality, the 'richest' 1 per cent of the population would receive 1 per cent of total incomes, the 'richest' 5 per cent would receive 5 per cent of all incomes, and so on. The Table shows that there were considerable deviations from equality. In the UK the richest 1 per cent of income earners received 6 per cent of all incomes so that their share was slightly greater than the comparable group in the Federal Republic of Germany and Ireland, but less than in the USA. If the top 5 per cent are considered, the position in the UK, Germany, and Ireland was very similar, though again the USA had a much more unequal distribution of income.

If we look at the other end of the income scale, the poorest 20 per cent of the population received only 3 per cent or 4 per cent of total incomes in the USA or Germany, but 8 per cent or 9 per cent in Ireland and the UK.

Note that this Table is concerned with incomes. The distribution of *wealth* may be very different.

Explanations of the Distribution of Income

There is no completely satisfactory explanation of the distribution of income, but a variety of reasons have been suggested. These include:

(1) Differences in wealth give rise to differences in income because rich people receive interest on their investments. Therefore to explain inequalities of income, we need to explain inequalities of wealth.

(2) Different countries have less or more generous systems of trans-
fer payments such as pensions and social security benefits.

(3) Different tax systems will affect the distribution of income after
tax.

(4) Different distributions of income arise from work because of
factors such as:

  (*a*) the different mixtures of occupations in different countries;

  (*b*) the influence of levels of education and social class patterns
  which vary between countries;

  (*c*) trade unions may have greater impact in some countries;
  and

  (*d*) 'monopoly' professions such as doctors or lawyers may
  restrict entry and so force up their earnings.

(5) Poorer countries have much more unequal distributions of
income than do richer countries.

Note that this section has been concerned with the *distribution* of
income rather than the *level* of incomes. To explain the latter it
would be necessary to explain how economies grow, a difficult task
which (fortunately for the authors) goes beyond the scope of this
chapter.

Incomes have been discussed in this section because they are an
important effect of work. The discussion of incomes also illustrates
some of the problems faced by social scientists in measuring and
comparing data which at first glance might not be seen as problems
at all.

Concept Box 2.3 Social Class

No society is composed of equals: social stratification is found in
every society. In advanced capitalist economies certain common
patterns can be found, though the rigidities of class patterns may be
greater in some societies than in others. The importance of these
divisions is enormous, for example:

(1) There are significant correlations (statistical links) between
social class and the following: infant mortality, reading ability,
height, access to university, defective vision, tooth decay,
number of books in the home, voting patterns, etc.

(2) More generally, the existence and consequences of social class may affect the whole way in which societies are run, the way change takes place, how conflict occurs and is resolved.

Despite the widespread use of the term 'social class' by social scientists and by others, there is a considerable amount of disagreement about the precise meaning of the term and about how classes should be distinguished. At a basic level it is possible to distinguish two alternative views that correspond to the Pluralist and Marxist perspectives. Pluralists tend to differentiate classes by occupation, whilst Marxists focus on the ownership of the means of production.

Incomes are an obvious consequence of work. What is less obvious but of vital concern to social scientists is the relationship between work and social class. From a Pluralist perspective different criteria such as education, life-style, birth, or income can be used to distinguish social classes. However, occupation is the most commonly used criterion and can be used to stratify people into a number of different classes. There are various ways in which this can be done. In Britain, the Registrar General and the Institute of Practitioners in Advertising both make use of occupations to categorize people, but there are slight differences between their categories:

Registrar General's Classification

No. Definition
1 Professional
2 Employers and managers
3 Intermediate and junior non-manual
4 Skilled manual (including foremen and supervisors) and own account non-professional
5 Semi-skilled manual and personal service
6 Unskilled manual

Institute of Practitioners in Advertising (IPA) Definition

Social class categories are based on head of household's occupation as follows:

Class A   Higher managerial, administrative, or professional

Class B   Intermediate managerial, administrative, or professional
Class C1   Supervisory or clerical, and junior managerial, adminis-
           trative, or professional
Class C2   Skilled manual workers
Class D   Semi and unskilled manual workers
Class E   State pensioners or widows (no other earners), casual or
           lowest grade work.

Whatever the criteria for distinguishing between classes, there are always problems in fitting particular occupations into their correct slot and borderlines between the classes are necessarily blurred. Despite its limitations, the kind of classification is particularly useful to researchers analysing the relationships between occupation and certain types of behaviour such as those discussed above. It is also useful to advertisers aiming at a specific target; for example readers of particular newspapers can be differentiated by social class and therefore advertisers can direct their efforts at specific groups.

Profile 2.2 Karl Marx (1818–1883)

His life

Karl Marx was born into a comfortable middle-class Jewish family in Germany. His father was an eminent lawyer who had converted to Christianity, largely to further his career. His mother was an unedu-cated, hard-working woman whose interests were largely confined to her husband and eight children.

Marx was educated at home until he was twelve and then he went to the local High School. When he left he came eighth out of thirty-two in his class, though he was a good deal younger than most of the others. At 17 he went to Bonn University to study law. He took an active part in student life—he was imprisoned for a night by the university for drun-kenness and he was wounded above the eye in a duel. Later he trans-ferred to Berlin University and in 1841 obtained a doctorate.

Whilst a young man he fell in love with a girl called Jenny who was descended from an aristocratic family, and because of her parents' opposition they did not marry until Marx was 25. It was a happy marriage—he used to write her love poems—and after thirteen years of marriage he wrote to her in a letter '. . . I have the living image of you in front of me, I hold you in my arms, kiss you from head to foot, fall before you on my knees and sigh "Madam I love you" '. They had five children but three of these died while Marx was still alive.

Marx's political views made it impossible for him to obtain a university post in Germany. He therefore turned to journalism and for the rest of his life writing was a principal source of income. The amounts he earned in this way were not large and the family income was often supplemented by gifts from his friend and collaborator Engels who was a manufacturer's son. Marx's finances were usually in chaos. This was partly due to his generosity—after his marriage to Jenny they kept money in a chest and left it open for their impecunious friends to help themselves. He was also extravagant—whilst he was a student his father complained 'As though we were made of gold my gentleman son disposes of almost 700 thalers in a single year . . . whereas the richest spend no more than 500.'

Later they were forced to sell all their possessions to pay the landlord and in 1852 Marx wrote 'Already for a week I have been in the pleasant position of not going out because my coat is in the pawnshop and of not being able to eat meat because of lack of credit.' In the same year he had to borrow money to bury his daughter. To alleviate their poverty Marx applied for a post on the railways but was rejected because of his handwriting! Despite these financial problems they had the help of a maid who came from Jenny's mother and who stayed with them all their lives.

For several years Marx lived in Paris and Brussels, taking an active part in politics and writing for various newspapers. However, in 1849 he moved to London which remained his home for the rest of his life.

He spent much of his time writing newspaper articles to raise money, and books and articles on many areas of social science. These needed extensive research in the library of the British Museum. He was also active in left-wing political organizations, though he found these time-consuming.

He once gave an account of himself in the parlour game 'Confessions':

Favourite virtue	Simplicity
Favourite virtue in men	Strength
Favourite virtue in women	Weakness
Your idea of happiness	To fight
Your idea of misery	Submission
Favourite occupation	Book-worming
Favourite colour	Red
Favourite dish	Fish

His wife Jenny died in 1881, in the Spring of 1883 his eldest daughter died, and Marx followed in March. He is buried in Highgate cemetery.

His thought

It is impossible to give a universally acceptable account of Marx's thought because it was so complex and far-reaching. Moreover there are as many varieties of Marxism as there are of Christianity and each claims to represent the true Marx.

To over-simplify greatly, Marx took German philosophy, English economics, and French politics and transformed them into something unique. Thus it is possible to trace the origins of some of his ideas in philosophy to Hegel, and he became a socialist whilst in France. The originality of his thought lies in his efforts to master the entire legacy of social thought since Aristotle and to use this knowledge to create a science of society.

From his extensive historical studies he concluded that capitalism would be followed by a transitory stage of socialism and ultimately by communism.

The essential feature of any society was the mode of production which it used. These modes of production determine the class structure which was the impelling force leading to revolution. Capitalism represents the last stage in this class struggle. It has created enormous wealth which if used rationally could ensure material well-being for all. But it cannot do this because its very nature is competitive, and therefore it is characterized by misery and conflict.

In capitalist society the capitalists own the means of production and the workers are forced to sell their labour in order to live. Because they own economic power the capitalists also control political power. The institutions of society—the law, media, police, church, education—may seem to be independent, but in practice they serve the interest of the owners of capital. Thus the education system socializes people into accepting capitalist values—that profit is good, that hard work is necessary, that we should obey those in authority. It also produces trained manpower which can be employed by the capitalists.

His importance

Marx's work has been used in two ways. First as an ideology which uses his ideas for political purposes expressed as a party doctrine which can be so dogmatic that Marx himself asserted 'I am not a Marxist.' In this way particular interpretations of his ideas have had an enormous impact on the lives of millions of people in countries such as the USSR.

The second way his ideas have been influential is through scholarly activity in social science. His ideas have had a huge influence in several disciplines. It is probably no exaggeration to call him the dominant figure in social science for the last century.

He introduced many new concepts such as *alienation* (discussed in the text) and *the reserve army of labour* which views the unemployed as a creation of the capitalists in order to keep down the wages of those in work. Above all, his concept of class and his emphasis on the social relations of production as a determining factor have illuminated subsequent analyses of the whole society and of groups, institutions, and beliefs within society.

Further reading

David McLellan (1973). *Karl Marx: His Life and Thought*. London: Granada gives a full account. The same author has written *Fontana Modern Masters* books on *Marx* and *Engels*. There are many books dealing with particular aspects of his work, e.g. R. Freedman (ed.) (1962). *Marx on Economics*. Harmondsworth: Penguin. However, many of these are rather difficult.

An alternative analysis of class is that of Karl Marx. This is a complex and controversial area of social science where simplification is difficult to achieve without distortion. The most straightforward approach is to quote from *The Communist Manifesto*, written by Marx and Engels in 1848 and this is done in Document 2.1.

Document 2.1 The Communist Manifesto (Extract)

The history of all hitherto existing society is the history of class struggles.

Freeman and slave, patrician and plebian, lord and serf, guild master and journeyman, in a word oppressor and oppressed, stood in constant opposition to one another, carried on an uninterrupted, now hidden, now open fight, a fight that each time ended, either in a revolutionary reconstruction of society at large, or in the common ruin of the contending classes.

In the earlier epochs of history, we find almost everywhere a complicated arrangement of society into various orders, a manifold graduation of social rank. In ancient Rome we have patricians, knights, plebians, slaves; in the Middle Ages, feudal lords, vassals, guild master, journeymen, apprentices, serfs; in almost all of these classes, again, sub-ordinate graduations.

The modern bourgeois society that has sprouted from the ruins of feudal society has not done away with class antagonisms. It has but established new classes, new conditions of oppression, new forms of struggle in place of the old ones!

Our epoch, the epoch of the bourgeoisie, possesses however this distinctive feature; it has simplified the class antagonisms. Society as a whole is splitting up into two great hostile camps, into two great classes facing each other—bourgeoisie and proletariat . . .

The bourgeoisie during its rule of scarce one hundred years, has created more massive and more colossal productive forces than have all preceeding generations put together. Subjection of nature's forces to man, machinery, application of chemistry to industry and agriculture, steam navigation railways, electric telegraphs, clearing of whole continents for cultivation, canalization of rivers, whole populations conjured out of the ground—what earlier century had even a presentiment that such productive forces slumbered in the lap of social labour? . . .

In proportion as the bourgeoisie, i.e. capital, is developed, in the same proportion is the proletariat, the modern working class developed, a class of labourers, who live only as long as they find work, and who find work only so long as their labour increases capital.

Source: Marx and Engels 1848, sect. 1.

These extracts show that for Marx, social class was determined by economic forces. The crucial distinction between the two main classes was the ownership of the means of production such as factories. The bourgeoisie owns the means of production, and it receives the surplus value created by the workers in the form of profits. In other words, the value of the labourer to the capitalist is greater than the wages paid to him.

The workers, or proletariat as Marx called them, are forced to sell their labour in order to live, so that work is not really voluntary but is forced and is merely a means for satisfying other needs. Moreover, workers do not own or control what they produce. Consequently workers do not find satisfaction in their work: they are alienated from it. By *alienation*, Marx means that workers lose control over the processes of work and the product of their labour and become depersonalized objects so that interpersonal relations are characterized by calculation and selfishness.

The proletariat and the bourgeoisie both depend on each other and are antagonistic to each other. They depend on each other because the owners need workers and the workers need employment. Their relations are antagonistic because the bourgeoisie seeks to keep down wages whilst the workers want to increase them.

According to Marx, the result is inevitable. As industry develops workers cease to be isolated but are forced to work together in large factories. This association leads to the development of *class consciousness*, which eventually unites the working class. This class is also strengthened because competition between capitalists concentrates power in fewer and fewer hands forcing more and more of the bourgeoisie to go bankrupt and to become workers: 'The development of modern industry, therefore, cuts from under its feet the very foundation on which the bourgeoisie produces and appropriates products. What the bourgeoisie therefore produces, above all, are its own grave diggers. Its fall and the victory of the proletariat are equally inevitable.' (Marx and Engels 1848, sect. 1.) In other words, the very development of capitalism leads to its destruction because capital becomes concentrated in fewer and fewer hands, profits fall, the workers become more united and overthrow capitalism which is replaced by a socialist system, where most of the means of production are held in common ownership and which in turn will be replaced by a classless communist society.

This outline provides a simplistic version of Marx's view of class, which in turn is part of a more general theory of how societies develop and change. Moreover as outlined here it does not account for the reality of modern capitalism in a number of ways:

- It makes no mention of the 'middle classes'. People such as managers form an important group in a modern economy. Though they do not own the means of production they have power to make decisions.

- In modern economies there is often a separation of ownership from control. Most shares in companies are owned by pension funds and insurance companies who invest on behalf of their subscribers, but they take very few economic decisions in the companies whose shares they own.

- There are many divisions *within* the proletariat and *within* the bourgeoisie; for example skilled workers may have conflicting interests to those who are unskilled.

• Social divisions based on sex and race may be more important than those based on class.

Modern Marxists would argue that his theories do take account of factors such as these, and can be adapted to analyse changing circumstances. They would argue that ownership of wealth is still highly concentrated, that possession of wealth in the form of houses or pension rights gives little power to the workers and that control remains concentrated in the hands of a few owners of private capital. The livelihood of those who do not own capital is set by the terms they can get for their work in the labour market. Moreover they would argue that inequalities of race and sex *derive* from and reinforce class divisions. The ultimate demise of capitalism is inevitable for Marxists, and they would argue that the signs of this can be found in the periodic crises which occur in all capitalist countries and which are most clearly visible in the figures for unemployment.

What is Unemployment?

The problem of defining unemployment

As we have seen earlier, the search for precise meanings is important in social science because it is easy for different people to mean different things by the same word. If comparisons are to be made, or data are to be analysed, then it is necessary for everyone to be clear about what is being analysed. Thus if we want to compare unemployment in several countries, or with the past, then the first step is to find out precisely what the data measure. In the case of unemployment it may seem obvious that someone is unemployed when they want a job and can't get one. In practice it is not easy to be so precise, because people don't want *any* job, they may want a job at a reasonable wage in a particular area. This means that it may be difficult to decide if someone is unemployed. For example, which of the following are unemployed:

(a) a divorced woman with two children, one at school, one at a part-time playgroup, who would like a part-time job;

(b) a sixty-two year old retired person receiving a pension who is bored and would like an interesting part-time job near home;

(c) a severely handicapped person who would take any job, but whose handicap makes any job extremely unlikely;

(*d*) the members of a farmer's family who work on the farm but receive no pay;

(*e*) a fifty-year-old who built up a business, sold it, and now lives on the interest and who would like an interesting job at a suitable salary but is not willing to work otherwise;

(*f*) a self-employed person such as a plumber with no work at the moment;

(*g*) a school-leaver on a short-term job creation/training project; and

(*h*) a student on vacation who would like a job for a few weeks before college starts again?

It is possible to have legitimate disagreement as to which of the above is unemployed and it is possible to have more than one acceptable definition to 'unemployment'. However, if people do use different definitions, then it is impossible to answer even simple questions such as 'Is unemployment higher in country A or in country B?'. In order to make such comparisons, a generally acceptable definition is needed. In order to solve this problem for unemployment, an international conference of labour statisticians met and agreed on a definition of unemployment.

Document 2.2 The Definition of Unemployment

(1) Persons in unemployment consist of all persons above a specified age who, on the specified day or for a specified week, were in the following categories:

(*a*) workers available for employment whose contract of employment had been terminated or temporarily suspended and who were without a job and seeking work for pay or profit;

(*b*) persons who were available for work (except for minor illness) during the specified period and were seeking work for pay or profit, who were never previously employed or whose most recent status was other than that of employee (i.e. former employers, etc.), or who had been in retirement;

(c) persons without a job and currently available for work who had made arrangements to start a new job at a date subsequent to the specified period.

(2) The following categories of persons are not considered to be unemployed:

(a) persons intending to establish their own business or farm, but who had not yet arranged to do so, who were not seeking work for pay or profit;

(b) former unpaid family workers not at work and not seeking work for pay or profit.

Source: ILO 1976, p. 1.

Although Document 2.2 gives an 'official' definition, it does not really solve the problem because it still has to be decided if a person is really 'seeking work for pay or profit.' As many of the examples above indicate, people are often not looking for any job at any rate of pay, but for particular types of work in particular areas at 'suitable' rates of pay. There is therefore room for considerable disagreement as to whether a person is actually 'seeking work for pay or profit.'

This example of an official definition is unusual in the social sciences. Frequently individual researchers prepare their own definitions or, where official statistics are concerned, the definition may vary between countries.

The problem of measuring unemployment

Even where these difficulties of definition are sorted out, the problem remains of actually counting the unemployed. This is exactly the same kind of problem that was found in trying to obtain details of people's incomes. There is no equivalent of a thermometer available to measure unemployment, and governments—or social scientists—have to develop a variety of techniques in order to obtain data. In the case of unemployment there are two main ways in which this is done.

The first method makes use of sample surveys of the labour force. In other words, the government carries out a survey similar to those which are used to predict voting in elections. A sample of people are asked questions such as 'Are you without work and seeking a job?'

This type of survey is used in Australia, Canada, Japan, and the USA.

The second way in which unemployment statistics are obtained is to make use of administrative records such as unemployment office statistics where people who are looking for work register so that they can be put in touch with employers or obtain unemployment benefits. This method of obtaining statistics is used in a variety of countries including France, the Federal Republic of Germany, New Zealand, Nigeria, and the UK.

It is clear that comparisons are difficult between countries where different techniques are used to obtain the statistics, particularly when the techniques vary so much. What is also true, but less obvious, is that accurate comparisons are not easy even between countries using the same method. To give just two examples:

(1) The age at which people can be considered unemployed varies between countries—in Chile it is twelve, in Canada fifteen, and in the USA sixteen years.

(2) In the case of labour registration statistics, people may or may not register even if they are looking for work. In the UK, for example, people are only counted if they are entitled to benefit. Individuals who want work but are not eligible for benefit do not count as unemployed. This applies to many married women who have not contributed to the insurance scheme.

The rather extensive discussion of the problems of definition and measurement of unemployment—and earlier of income—has been undertaken for two reasons. First, because the problems are relevant to any discussion of people considered as workers. And second, as Method Box 2.1 showed, this is a widespread problem in social science. Hardly any social variables have universally acceptable definitions or are easy to measure. Whether we are talking about housing, stress, poverty, or love, a wide variety of definitions and methods of measurement are possible.

The difficulties that are faced in defining and measuring unemployment are therefore typical of those faced by social scientists in many other areas. Indeed those wishing to make international comparisons of employment are relatively fortunate, because statisticians have undertaken studies which make the figures for individual countries more comparable. They do this by using one set of figures such as those for the USA as a standard and then adjusting others.

Figures adjusted in this way to show the unemployment rate in a selection of countries are shown in Table 2.2.

Three things are apparent from these statistics. First, there is never a time when unemployment is completely absent. Second, some countries have persistently higher unemployment rates than others. Third, it is clear that unemployment rates tend to rise and fall together across countries, so that all countries tend to experience high levels of unemployment at more or less the same time. Any theory seeking to explain unemployment, and any policies to reduce unemployment must take account of these patterns.

The effects of unemployment

Being unemployed is not the same as having abundant leisure. One is voluntary, the other is not. Moreover the effects are very different. An abundance of leisure time may open up choice to the individual while unemployment may do the reverse.

It is difficult to be precise about the effects of unemployment. Not only will they vary from person to person, but there is no perfect way to discover people's experiences.

One method is to do the obvious; that is to ask the unemployed to describe their feelings. One disadvantage of this approach is that it is impossible to question all the unemployed so that those who are approached may not give a true impression of the whole. The unemployed may be unable or unwilling to answer the questions and the interviewer's own beliefs and values may affect the way the statements are interpreted. Just as partisan spectators at a football match disagree about what they see, so social science investigators are liable to interpret the evidence to support their existing point of view.

Despite these limitations, interviews are a major source of knowledge about how people feel and sometimes this information can be combined with more 'objective' evidence such as statistics. For example, one obvious effect of unemployment is that incomes fall. This can be measured using official figures for unemployment benefit and discussed in conjunction with information obtained from interviewees.

However, the most important effects may not be financial but social and psychological and here statistical data may not be available. The words of the unemployed themselves may be the best evidence.

One investigation of the effects of unemployment suggested that

Table 2.2. Percentage Unemployment Rates

	1973	1974	1975	1976	1977	1978	1979	1980	1981	1982	1983	1984
Australia	2.3	2.7	4.9	4.8	5.7	6.3	6.2	6.1	5.8	7.2	10.0	9.0
Canada	5.6	5.4	6.9	7.1	8.1	8.4	7.5	7.5	7.6	11.0	11.9	11.3
France	2.6	2.8	4.1	4.4	4.7	5.2	5.9	6.3	7.3	8.0	8.0	9.7
FRG	1.2	2.6	4.7	4.6	4.5	4.3	3.8	3.8	5.5	7.5	9.1	9.1
Hong Kong	—	—	9.1	5.6	4.3	2.9	2.9	3.8	3.9	3.8	4.5	3.9
Ireland	7.2	7.9	12.2	12.3	11.8	10.7	9.3	10.3	13.5	16.5	20.8	—
Japan	1.3	1.4	1.9	2.0	2.0	2.2	2.1	2.0	2.2	2.4	2.6	2.7
New Zealand	0.2	0.1	0.4	0.4	0.6	1.8	2.0	2.9	3.6	3.9	5.7	5.0
UK	2.6	2.6	4.0	5.5	5.8	5.7	5.3	6.8	10.4	12.1	12.9	13.1
USA	4.9	5.6	8.3	7.6	7.9	6.0	5.8	7.0	7.5	9.5	9.5	7.4

Note: In order to understand a table such as this, concentrate first on the main change for each country—has unemployment risen and roughly by how much e.g. has it doubled? Then compare countries: which countries have high unemployment levels, which have low? Then analyse patterns e.g. unemployment rose almost everywhere in 1975—a graph type sketch is one way to do this.

Source: Year Book of Labour Statistics (1984) Table 9, International Labour Organization, Geneva.

the unemployed went through three phases (Hill 1978). Although the first phase can be traumatic, people often feel that they can be enjoyably idle or do more jobs around the house. An unemployed restaurateur reported his feelings: 'that's great, I can lie in the morning, get up, sit down, go and wash the car and go for a little walk.'

However, any euphoria soon disappears and the unemployed become bored and depressed: 'I sit at home and can't be bothered to watch television . . . it's so depressing—I get more and more depressed sitting indoors—there's nothing to do', reported an unemployed trainee nurse.

After a time the unemployed may settle down to accept their situation and new status. Active search for work may cease or become infrequent. The individual adjusts to the situation. 'I've adapted but I don't want to adapt', said one man. 'You could easily stay like that. I could be on the dole for the rest of my life.'

The research concluded: 'The loss of a job diminishes confidence. This reduces effective social contacts outside the home and focuses tension within the family. In turn, this reduces the support the family can give and so reduces confidence still further.' (p. 119)

There are exceptions to this pattern. Some feel released from a boring routine and use their enforced leisure constructively, but for most people unemployment is a major problem.

What can be done about unemployment?

It is clear that there is no easy solution to the problem of unemployment; if there were, governments would take the measures which were necessary to eradicate it and unemployment would cease to exist. Table 2.2 suggests that even when economies are booming there will be some people who are unemployed. Most of these will be suffering from what economists call *frictional* unemployment. As its name suggests this occurs when people are slow to move between jobs and are out of work for a short period between jobs. Frictional unemployment is not really a serious problem if people obtain new work fairly quickly.

Much more important is *structural* unemployment which occurs when the structure of industry changes—for example, when a coal mine becomes exhausted, a process or product becomes obsolete, or an industry finds that it cannot compete with newer producers. In cases such as this the cause may be obvious, but the cure is difficult. Although some countries are more liable to suffer from structural unemployment than others because of their particular industrial make-up, the impact of structural unemployment is often concentrated in particular regions. For example, the steel industries in Europe and the USA faced increasing competition from Japan and other countries in the 1970s and were forced to close down the steel plants, often with severe effects on the local community. Governments may try to lure new industries to these areas, but there are only a limited number of firms looking for new sites. They may also seek to retrain workers for new skills or encourage them to move to areas where jobs are available. Neither process is easy. Family ties and housing difficulties make geographical mobility difficult and it is not always easy to acquire new skills.

However, the most serious kind of unemployment is that which exists on a mass scale, affecting large numbers of people in many industries throughout the economy. This kind of unemployment spreads across national frontiers and is the main reason why high unemployment is found at the same time in many countries. For Marxists this kind of unemployment provides an example of the crises which they regard as inevitable in a capitalist society. For non-Marxists, and for Western governments searching for policies to combat this type of unemployment, the most influential analysis is that of an English economist, John Maynard Keynes. His work can be used to exemplify a technique used by many social scientists—that of building a model.

Method Box 2.2 Building a Model

The world is too complex for anyone to comprehend it fully, so social scientists extract from this complexity by picking out the points which they think are important and then analysing the relationships between these points. In doing this they are merely doing formally what we all do in everyday life. To get from home to work I have a mental model in my head which tells me where to turn and which roads I can ignore. In the same way geographers constructing maps are making visual models. No map contains every feature of the landscape; the mapmakers select certain features such as hills and roads which they feel are important and then incorporate them, on a smaller scale, on the map. They ignore many features—weeds, litter, shrubs, people—which they feel are not relevant. When the map is completed it can be put to operational use—for example, to work out directions between places.

There are many other types of model. Diagrammatic models are used by scientists of all kinds—an electrical circuit diagram by physicists, for example. Social psychologists may show diagrammatically the patterns of interaction in a group. More sophisticated models can be represented mathematically.

Models, then, are idealized abstractions from reality; they ignore some features and concentrate on others which are believed to be significant, and they come in many forms—verbal, diagrammatic, and mathematical.

Profile 2.3 John Maynard Keynes (1883–1946)

His life

Keynes' family background was academic. His father was an economist and administrator at Cambridge University and his mother was also a graduate who became the first woman councillor in Cambridge. He had a happy childhood in a secure home background. He went to a preparatory school where he won a scholarship to Eton and in 1902 he progressed to King's College, Cambridge to read Mathematics. Though he was twelfth in his class he obtained first-class honours. He then took the Civil Service entrance examinations—where the examiners thought his worst subjects were mathematics and economics! For a short time he worked in the India Office before returning to King's College as a Fellow.

During the First World War he worked in the Treasury, though he resigned from his position in protest at the harshness of the Peace Treaty and wrote a book, *The Economic Consequences of the Peace*. Keynes could be arrogant and vituperative: he called the British Prime Minister Lloyd George 'this goat-footed bard, this half-human visitor to our age from the hag ridden magic and enchanted woods of Celtic antiquity.'

Whilst a student at Cambridge, Keynes developed his interest in the arts, and these remained a lifelong passion. Whilst a Treasury official he started the British National Gallery's collection of modern French paintings, and later he founded the Cambridge Arts Theatre, and the Arts Council of Great Britain.

Although as a young man he had several homosexual experiences he married a Russian ballerina in 1925 and enjoyed a stable marriage. At parties they would dance together a version of the cancan which they called the Keynes-Keynes. He was an active member of the Bloomsbury set along with other writers and artists including E. M. Forster, Virginia Woolf, and Bertrand Russell who wrote, 'Keynes' intellect was the sharpest and clearest I have ever known. When I argued with him I felt that I took my life in my hands and I seldom emerged without feeling something of a fool.'

He enjoyed arguments: Churchill to Keynes: 'Am coming round to your point of view.' Keynes to Churchill: 'Sorry to hear it; have started to change my mind!' He was a non-conformist in that he challenged old beliefs and insisted on *his* right to make moral judgements. Thus, although his job exempted him from military service, in the First World War, he wrote requesting exemption because 'I have a conscientious objection to surrendering my liberty of judgement on so vital a question as undertaking military service.'

During the Second World War he worked in the Treasury again and was largely responsible for British economic policy. Towards the end of the war he was the leading figure in negotiations at Bretton Woods which led to the formation of the International Monetary Fund and the World Bank and which provided an institutional framework for postwar prosperity.

Keynes's health was never good. He had several heart attacks and died from one of these on Easter Sunday 1946.

His ideas

Keynes's most important theory is outlined in the text. It is the prime example of his belief that economists should seek to remedy the economic problems faced by society. At a banquet he gave a toast to 'economics and economists who are the trustees—not of civilisation—but of the possibilities of civilisation.' The essence of his position was that human beings could use rational thought to analyse society and then make use of the institutions of society—such as government—to improve life. Thus Keynes believed that the government should take an active interventionist role in the economy.

He was a prolific writer—the Royal Economic Society has published his collected works in thirty substantial volumes. In addition to economics he wrote about politics and the arts. He was less interested in ideas for their own sake than in using ideas to change things for the better.

His importance

As an economist Keynes has dominated the last fifty years. A young economist of the time called Samuelson who later won the Nobel Prize wrote of Keynes's stunning impact on graduate students in 1936, 'Bliss was it in that dawn to be alive, but to be young was heaven.' It is still impossible to write about those aspects of economics which interested Keynes without being influenced by his arguments. Even those economists who reject his views usually begin by criticizing him. The biggest challenge to his supremacy came in the 1970s when a group of economists giving greater priority to inflation than to unemployment laid much greater emphasis on controlling the money supply and to restricting the role of government than had Keynesian economists.

His theories changed the way in which governments acted. A major reason for the growth in the economies of many countries after the Second World War was that his ideas were widely practised.

Ideas can change the world. As Keynes wrote, 'Practical men who believe themselves to be quite exempt from any intellectual influences, are usually the slave of some defunct economist. Madmen in authority who hear voices in the air are distilling their frenzy from some academic scribbler of a few years back . . . sooner or later it is ideas not vested interests which are dangerous for good or evil.'

Further reading

Almost all economics books dealing with government policy contain sections devoted to his ideas. Peter Donaldson (1984). *Economics of the Real World*. 3rd edn. Harmondsworth: Penguin is a well written introduction to economics. Biographies include R. Harrod (1951). *The Life of John Maynard Keynes*. London: Macmillan, and D. E. Moggridge (1976). *Keynes*. London: Macmillan.

Keynes's model may be shown in any number of ways, but the easiest is to approach it diagrammatically, though its original formulation in his book *The General Theory of Employment Interest and Money* (1936) was more complex.

The model assumes the economy has two sectors, households and firms, and money flows from households to firms when consumers spend money on goods and services. Money also flows from firms to households in the form of wages, rent, interest, and dividends. This is shown in figure 2.2. Clearly this model is grossly over-simplified and needs extending to make it more realistic. In order to do this we take account of various injections into the system and withdrawals from it. Thus some of the money received by households is not spent but is saved and so does not go to firms. Similarly, some of the money received by firms is kept by them in the form of retained

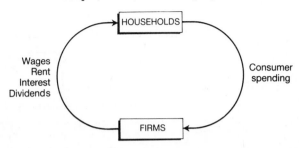

Fig. 2.2 The Circular Flow of Income

profits, which are a kind of saving by the firm. These are both withdrawals from the system.

Savings are not the only kind of withdrawal. If households buy goods from abroad—or go on foreign holidays—money is withdrawn from the system and goes abroad. In the same way government removes money from the system when it taxes individuals and firms. These withdrawals are shown in figure 2.3. The effect of these withdrawals is to reduce the circular flow of incomes; that is to lower incomes in the economy. If this were the complete picture the economy would soon collapse because each time the money flows round the system these withdrawals from the system reduce incomes which are needed to purchase goods and services.

However, there are also injections into the system. Firms may borrow from banks, or use their own savings to invest in new machines or buildings. This means that other firms receive money for supplying the equipment and so this injects money into the system and increases the circular flow. Another injection into the system occurs when firms sell goods or services (such as insurance) to

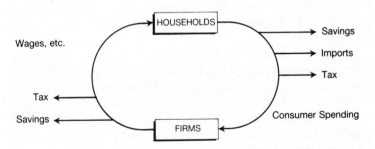

Fig. 2.3 Withdrawals from the Circular Flow of Income

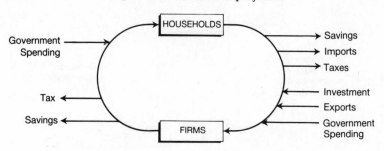

Fig. 2.4 Withdrawals and Injections into the System

other countries and so receive money from foreign consumers. Finally, both firms and households receive money from government spending in a variety of ways such as wages, payments for goods or services, or as pensions. These injections increase the incomes received by firms and households. The full picture of injections and withdrawals is shown in figure 2.4. If injections are greater than withdrawals then the level of incomes in the economy will rise. If withdrawals are greater than injections then incomes will fall.

How does this Keynesian model of the economy relate to unemployment? Keynes argued that mass unemployment was caused by lack of sufficient *aggregate demand* for the goods and services produced by firms throughout the economy. To an economist 'demand' exists when people are willing and able to spend money on a commodity or service. The demand for cars or haircuts is the number that are actually bought. If the people who produce such goods or services could sell more, they would probably take on more workers and unemployment in these industries would fall. In the same way if aggregate demand—the demand for goods and services in the economy as a whole—could be increased, many employers would take on more workers to satisfy this demand and so reduce unemployment.

Therefore the way to reduce unemployment is to increase aggregate demand and that can be done by increasing the circular flow of income. If incomes of either firms or households rise, then more money will flow round the system, and so increase aggregate demand. Therefore in a Keynesian system a government faced with mass unemployment should increase the level of injections and/or reduce the level of withdrawals. As many of the variables are difficult for the government to influence, in practice this means that the government should increase its own spending and/or cut taxes. One result of this is that the government will spend more than it receives and will have to increase the quantity of money or to borrow the difference. As governments borrow all the time this is not necessarily a serious consequence. The analogy which is sometimes made which suggests that governments are like families or firms is false. A family which consistently spends more than it receives in income will soon run into trouble. Unless there is a total collapse of the system, governments can do this in perpetuity because there are always people willing to lend to the government.

However, there are difficulties involved in using the Keynesian model to run the economy. First, there may be a clash of objectives. The Keynesian solution to inflation (i.e. when there is a sustained rise in the general level of prices) is to cut government spending and to raise taxes in order to reduce excess incomes. The approach to unemployment is to do the reverse. There are therefore considerable difficulties when an economy is faced with both inflation and unemployment! In practice governments have to decide which objective should receive preference and concentrate on that whilst taking measures which mitigate the adverse effects on other objectives. Another difficulty arises because there are long time-lags and rigidities in the system. Measures which the government executes now may not have their full effect on the economy for many months when quite different measures may be required. Moreover the model as outlined above gives no indication of *how much* the variables should be increased or decreased. If government spending, for example, is increased by too much, the effect will be inflationary; if it is not increased enough, then unemployment will continue.

Because models are simplifications of reality they can never give a complete explanation of the system. They are judged by how well they seem to explain reality. In the case of models such as that of Keynes, they are judged by their usefulness—does the use of the Keynesian model reduce unemployment?

The question is easy to ask, but difficult to answer, and this is characteristic of many social science models. Reality is so complex that it is not possible to be conclusive about the validity of any particular model and that is one reason why social scientists so frequently disagree. There are two main ways in which a model such as this can be tested. The first is to translate the rather vague diagrams shown here into precise mathematical relationships and to feed into these relationships actual data on the economy. Then the predictions of the model can be compared with what happens in the real world. Mathematical models have been produced for a number of economies and Document 2.3 describes the Treasury model of the British economy.

Document 2.3 The Treasury Model of the British Economy

$$\text{LnXGMA} = 8.161 + (0.407 + 0.445g)\,\text{lnWT} + \sum_{i=0}^{18} a_i g^i\,\text{lnRWC}$$

$$+ \sum_{i=0}^{18} b_i g^i \ln(100.\text{UXGMA/pw}) - 0.00810\text{TXGM} + \sum_{i=0}^{10} c_i g^i\,\text{CBIBC}$$

The six hundred sums that add up to a forecaster's nightmare

An economist's laboratory is a sheet of paper; his model a set of mathematical equations. The market for economic forecast is crowded with different models, but the Treasury's is one of the biggest and the best known. It runs to about 600 equations. . . which predict the level of manufactured exports.

Models of this complication need computers to work out a forecast. But the model itself is not a machine, churning out automatic results. It is more like an animal, constantly growing and developing, which has to be fed, watered and massaged by the user.

The forecaster has to feed it with an enormous number of *assumptions* about things outside its scope—world trade, oil prices and so on. Then he has to supply it with information about the present. Next he has to tinker with the equations themselves. These seek to explain how one bit of the economy affects another—how, for example, companies will react if interest rates go up; how these reactions will affect employment; and so on, round the long but eventually circular economic chain.

But none of these reactions is totally predictable. The model's equations have to change, too, and contain *residuals*—dumping-grounds for bits of behaviour economists' theory cannot explain. Some *variables* such as wages or the exchange rate, are notoriously hard to 'model.'

Models are based on what happened in the past. So a model-user will have to make adjustments if he thinks things will be different in the future.

Models like the Treasury's are constantly changing, as their owners try to catch up with subtle changes in human behaviour. Today's Treasury model is not at all the same as the one first published six years ago. From time to time the Treasury publishes new versions of its model—and those who use it outside often alter the equations themselves. At any one moment, insiders and outsiders may be using rather different versions of the 'same' model.

A single forecast is usually the model user's best guess at the future. But if he wants to argue about the causes of growth or inflation, he will need to carry out *simulations*—extra exercises in which just one or two assumptions are changed. Simulations show differences: the amount by which output, unemployment, inflation, etc are higher or lower than in the main forecast.

Simulations will begin to tell you something about the economic judgements underlying the model. That is when the real argument can begin. Using a model is not a way of ending disagreement, but of being clearer and more consistent about where the causes of disagreement lie.

Source: Sunday Times 11 Apr. 1982.

One difficulty in this procedure is that in a mathematical model the relationships need to be specified precisely which can be done in different ways and so different results obtained. For example, if incomes of households increase by 5 per cent, how much of this will be saved? How much will be spent on imports? Differing answers to these questions may lead to quite different results even though the same basic model is used. Moreover, economic relationships vary over time. Equations which accurately explained economic behaviour in 1980 will not do so in 1990. The best example of this was the huge rise in oil prices in the 1970s. This affected many economic variables in ways which were impossible or difficult to predict by any model.

The second way in which an economic model can be tested is to see how it works in practice. In the present case, a model designed to reduce unemployment can perhaps be judged on how well it succeeds. On this criterion the evidence suggests that the Keynesian model was successful in keeping unemployment at very low levels in most developed economies from the Second World War to the 1970s. Since that time unemployment levels have risen, though whether this occurred because (*a*) the Keynesian model was unsuccessful or (*b*) governments did not make use of the model or made poor use of it, is a matter for argument. The rise in oil prices caused many governments to give greater priority to reducing inflation and to achieve this they restricted increases in government spending.

Thus the Keynesian model, like all complex models, can never be evaluated precisely. Like all social science models it is a simplification of reality and so inadequate. Constructive criticism by other social scientists may serve to refine and improve the basic model, but over time basic relationships in the economy will alter so that no social science model will ever achieve perfection.

Conclusion

Work can be a chore. Cries of 'Thank God it's Friday' fill the land each week. For those without it who would like it, work is something to be desired. For social scientists of all disciplines it is a fascinating subject to be studied. This chapter has focused on just a few aspects of work. Social science methods such as clear measurement and model building have been used to examine one major theory of how the problem of unemployment may be tackled.

References

Booth, F. (1980). *Robert Raikes of Gloucester*. Redhill: National Christian Education Council.

Gould, J. and W. L. Kolb (eds.) (1964). *A Dictionary of the Social Sciences*. London: Tavistock.

Hill, J. (1978). 'The Psychological Impact of Unemployment'. *New Society* 19 Jan., pp. 118 f.

I L O (1976). *International Recommendations on Labour Statistics*. Geneva.

Jahoda, M. (1979). 'The Psychological Meanings of Unemployment'. *New Society* 6 Sept., pp. 492 f.

Keynes, J. M. (1919) *Economic Consequences of the Peace*. London: Macmillan.

—— (1936) *The General Theory of Employment, Interest, and Money*. London: Macmillan.

Marx, K. and F. Engels (1848). *The Communist Manifesto*. London.

Thomlinson, R. (1965). *Sociological Concepts and Research*. New York: Random House.

Weber, M. (1930). *The Protestant Ethic and the Spirit of Capitalism*, trans. T. Parsons. London: Allen & Unwin.

Further Reading

There are innumerable introductions to economics but perhaps the most readable are those by Peter Donaldson whose (1984) *Economics of the Real World* 3rd edn. Harmondsworth: Penguin is a well-written survey. Colin Harbury (1981). *Descriptive Economics* 6th edn. London: Pitman focuses on the central features of the British economy with little reference to theory.

Two useful books on work from a sociological perspective are Robert Dubin (ed.) (1976). *Handbook of Work, Organizations, and Society*. Chicago: Rand McNally and Craig R. Littler (ed.) (1985). *The Experience of Work*. Aldershot: Gower whilst Michael Haralambos (ed.) (1983). *Sociology: A New Approach*. Ormskirk: Causeway Press has a useful chapter on 'Work and Leisure'.

3 Citizens in a Liberal Democracy

Citizenship is important. After the Second World War thousands of people became 'stateless persons'. Many were born in one country, then their homeland was occupied by Germany and eventually incorporated in the USSR. Thousands left their homes to avoid the fighting and found themselves citizens of nowhere.

Perhaps even more tragic are those who are denied citizenship in their own country. It is only when we are denied citizenship that we fully realize just how important it is. For many years, in many countries, Jews were denied the rights (and the duties) of citizenship in the countries in which they were born. In South Africa the majority of the population—the blacks—have been not been allowed to become full citizens of the country in which they live, work, and die.

Despite its importance, citizenship is a relatively neglected area of social science, though the topic is prominent in countries such as the USA where almost all the population are immigrants or the descendants of immigrants. There, the processes involved in becoming a citizen are an important feature of many people's lives and teaching about citizenship has a recognized place in the school curriculum.

People as citizens has been chosen as one of the dimensions of people's lives considered in this book because the term citizen seems to summarize better than any other many important aspects of our lives about which the discipline of politics has considerable relevance. But in addition to examining the contribution that this discipline has to make, we shall also be considering the contribution of law and sociology. How these various social sciences relate to the analysis which follows will be explained at the end of the chapter.

In order to sharpen our consideration of this dimension of people's lives, the material that follows focuses on a question of paramount importance to it: what is the role of a citizen in a liberal democracy? In unravelling an answer to this question we shall look first of all at the meaning that has been given to the concept of 'citizen' itself. We shall then look at views on what the role of citizens ought to be and how this is transmitted within society. The concept of liberal democracy will also be considered in this context. Finally, the role that citizens do in fact play will be examined in the light of some of the empirical evidence on the subject.

Meaning of Citizenship

Citizenship is primarily a legal concept and this is reflected in the definition reproduced below. It is taken from one of the many dictionaries of social science which exist. They are often a more fruitful source of definition of terms used by social scientists than standard dictionaries which tend to be more concerned with the everyday usage of such terms.

Concept Box 3.1 Citizenship

Citizenship may be defined (a) as a status of relationship existing between a natural person and a political society, known as the state, by which the former owes allegiance and the latter protection. This status or relationship between the individual and the state is determined by municipal law, and recognized by the law of nations; (b) as the status of the citizen in a society based upon the rule of law and the principle of equality.

Source: Gould and Kolb (eds.) 1964, p. 88.

The transference of this concept of citizen into legal regulations is a very complex task and has beset constitutional lawyers in Britain throughout the present century. Document 3.1 attempts to illustrate the complex nature of the contemporary legal regulations governing citizenship in Britain.

Document 3.1 UK Law on Citizenship

Citizenship of the United Kingdom has been determined since 1 January 1983 by the 1981 British Nationality Act. The regulations are too complex to reproduce here but in brief the Act provides for three separate citizenships, each giving different rights with regard to living permanently in the United Kingdom and having free movement in and out of it. Full rights in this respect are held by those with *British Citizenship*. Those eligible for such status are: (i) those who were full citizens of the United Kingdom on 31 December 1982; (ii) children born in the UK on or after 1 February 1983 if one or other parent is a British citizen or is settled in the UK; (iii) other children living in the UK for the first ten years of life; and (iv) adults possessing other UK citizenships after five years' residence. Others can apply for British citizenship through naturalization.

The other two citizenships do not provide for the same rights of abode and free entry. They are: (a) *British Dependent Territories Citizenship* for people connected with the Dependencies (like Hong Kong, Bermuda, and Gibraltar); and (b) *British Overseas' Citizenship* for those citizens of the UK and Colonies who, before 1 January 1983, did not have the necessary connections for the other two forms of citizenship. The rest of the world's population would generally be regarded as *Foreign Nationals* although Commonwealth and Republic of Ireland citizens are recognized for certain purposes.

One way of elucidating the role that citizens ought to play is to follow up a little further the legal interest in citizenship. From this angle we find an emphasis on the rights and duties that the title of citizen gives to the individual. The *rights* of citizens are commonly to be found in written constitutions. Thus the first amendment to the USA constitution states that 'Congress shall make no law respecting an establishment of religion, or prohibiting the free exercise thereof; or abridging the freedom of speech, or of the press; or the right of the people peaceably to assemble and petition the Government for a redress of grievances.'

Constitutions which claim to define and protect citizens' rights are not peculiar to Western democracies. The 1977 constitution of the USSR, for example, deals with equality of citizens' rights and chapter 7 of the constitution lists some of those rights. Article 39 of chapter 7 of the USSR constitution reads as follows:

Citizens of the USSR enjoy in full the social, economic, political, and personal rights and freedoms proclaimed and guaranteed by the Constitution of the USSR and by Soviet Laws. The socialist system ensures enlargement of the rights and freedoms of citizens and continuous improvement of their living standards as social, economic, and cultural development programmes are fulfilled. Enjoyment by citizens of their rights and freedoms must not be to the detriment of the interests of society or the state, or infringe the rights of other citizens.

Despite some similarities there are considerable differences in what the constitution makers see as rights. In the USA the focus is on individual freedoms such as the rights to keep and bear arms, to speedy and public trials, and other legal safeguards. In contrast, the consitution of the USSR provides for the following rights: to work, housing, education, cultural benefits, and to associate in public organizations. However, these rights are limited if they infringe upon the collective rights of the state.

One way to safeguard human rights is for a country to embody them in a written constitution which contains procedures like referendums that make it very difficult to alter. If rights are incorporated in the constitution, then in principle at least they ought to be secure.

Some countries have no constitutional Bill of Rights. In the case of Britain there is no formal constitutional document, as such, and the laws which say how Britain is to be governed often have no special status. As Document 3.2 shows, parliament may extend freedoms or it may reduce them. The fear that politicians may pass laws restricting the liberties of the individual has led a number of people to campaign for a formal Bill of Rights for British citizens.

Document 3.2 Citizens' Rights in the UK

---

(1) The rights of the British citizen are not codified into statements of general principle like the clauses in the Preamble to the French 1946

Constitution . . . Nor are they guaranteed any greater legal sanctity than that enjoyed, for example, by a Lotteries and Gaming Act. These liberties are founded in the common law of the kingdom, or in statutes, and in either case they are interpreted by the ordinary courts of the country; and both these and subsequent judicial decisions thereon can be overriden or altered by subsequent parliamentary statutes. In a word: the rights of. the British citizen are not 'entrenched'.

(2) Furthermore, these rights are residual. To know one's rights is to know what matters or actions the law forbids. Thus a citizen is free to express his opinion in speech or writing or other visual means subject, however, to a long train of restrictions including, *inter alia*, the laws relating to treason, the Official Secrets Act, sedition, defamation, incitement to mutiny or to disaffection, obscene publication or blasphemy; and to those also that relate to incitement to a criminal offence, or to provoking public discord or incitement to racial hatred. And each of these qualifying restrictions is defined by statute, common law, and the judicial decisions thereon.

(3) Finally, for every wrongful encroachment on the citizens' liberties, there exists a legal remedy, ascertainable and enforceable by the ordinary courts of the land.

Source: Finer 1979, pp. 83–4.

The law is therefore of central importance for determining who are, or are not, recognized as citizens of a particular country. But we need to go beyond this in order to gain an understanding of how this dimension of people's lives affects what is expected of them in terms of their relationship with the state and the part that they actually play in its affairs. In considering what is expected of citizens we need to examine the normative issues involved. By normative in this context is meant examination of the values and ideas that have been attached to the concept of citizenship and in particular those about what ought to be expected of the citizen. In contrast to this, consideration of the actual part that citizens play in the affairs of the state requires examination of the empirical issues. Empirical issues refer to the facts of the matter and require us to look at the evidence that has been gathered on what the role of the citizen is in practice. Separation of the normative 'ought' question from the empirical 'is' question is one of the ways in which social science endeavours to search for objectivity. Only by making this separation is it then possible to be clearer about the ways in which a greater match can be achieved between 'theory' and practice.

Normative Issues

In political philosophy there seems to be considerable agreement from those of all shades of opinion that there are two interconnected requirements of citizens. As representative of this agreement we can take the following quotation from D. W. Brogan:

> The first—possibly the most important, certainly the most novel—aspect is the assumption that every citizen [has] the right to be consulted on the conduct of the political society and the duty of having something to contribute to the general consultation. The second aspect is the converse of the first. The citizen who has the right to be consulted is bound by the results of the consultation. His duties flow from his right. (Brogan 1960, pp. 4–5)

For purposes of our discussion here these dual requirements of the citizen are summarized as: (1) to be obedient to the state; and (2) to participate in its affairs.

It has been argued that these two requirements of obedience and participation are derived from values first developed in classical Greece and traditional Hebraic society. From classical Greece comes the notion of participation. Indeed the Greek word for citizen—'polites'—can be translated as 'a full participant in the common life of the community.' From the Hebraic tradition—and particularly the writings of the Old Testament—comes an emphasis on loyalty and service to the state. This Hebraic tradition was later absorbed and imparted to other civilizations by Imperial Rome. Although the two requirements of citizens have been traced to different historical traditions, both were clearly distinguished within the thought of one of the earliest of all political philosophers—Aristotle. The quotation in Document 3.3 is typical of Aristotle's writing and can be taken as typifiying, with its concern to clarify concepts, the philosophical approach to our question.

Document 3.3 Aristotle and the Idea of a
Good Citizen

. . . A citizen is one of a community, as a sailor is one of a crew; and
although each member of the crew has his own function and a name to fit
it—rower, helmsman, look-out, and the rest—and has therefore his goodness at that particular job, there is also a type of goodness which all the
crew must have, a function in which they all play a part—the safe conduct
of the voyage; for each member of the crew aims at securing that.
Similarly the aim of all the citizens, however dissimilar they may be, is the
safety of the community, that is, the constitution of which they are
citizens. . . . I think that we might say that the goodness of the citizen is
just this—to know well how to rule and be ruled . . . and the good citizen
must have the knowledge and ability both to rule and be ruled.

Source: Aristotle, *The Politics* Bk. III Chap. 4 (Sinclair 1962), pp. 107–10.

Profile 3.1 Aristotle (384–322 BC)

His life

Aristotle was born in the year 384 BC in a Greek city near to Macedonia
called Stagira. The son of a doctor, he became a pupil of Plato at the
age of 17 and remained so for a period of twenty years. Following the
death of Plato, Aristotle turned to travel and for a while became the
tutor of Alexander, the son of King Philip of Macedonia. When the
Macedonians advanced on Greece in later years this connection
forced Aristotle to leave Athens in 323 BC, a move which was followed
by his death a year later. For some twelve years prior to these events
Aristotle was the head of a school he had established in the Lyceum at
Athens.

His work

Aristotle's various writings are essentially based on the courses he
gave at his Lyceum school. Taken as a whole his works span an
enormous range of knowledge: logic, physics, biology, psychology,
pure philosophy, moral philosophy, literary criticism, and political
philosophy. He can indeed be seen as the founding father of these
subjects as separate areas of study.

His importance

Aristotle's writing became generally known from the thirteenth century onwards and were to have a widespread influence on medieval thought. His influence waned, however, with the development of modern scientific ideas from the seventeenth century onwards. In terms of his contribution to the social sciences his *Politics* is the most relevant work. This provides insights into what we would now recognize as economics and sociology, but mostly it is concerned, as the title suggests, with political aspects of society. The earliest part deals mainly with the general principles (including some conceptualization of the ideal state), while the later parts examine the structure of government as informed by an analysis of 158 separate constitutions. In these fields, his major impact on subsequent political ideas has been to see man as a political animal and to show how different forms of government can be classified. Aristotle's classification is based on three criteria—how many people rule the state, by whom, and in whose interests. The resulting categories can be shown as follows:

Number of Rulers	Social Groups	Rule in General Interest	Rule in self-interest
One	King	MONARCHY	TYRANNY
Few	Wealthy	ARISTOCRACY	OLIGARCHY
Many	Poor	POLITY	DEMOCRACY

It is of interest to note that Aristotle saw democracy as the 'perverted' form of a polity. His personal preference was for an aristocracy.

Further reading

A number of editions of *Politics* exist with different introductions and annotations. There is an extract from the Penguin edition translated by T. A. Sinclair in Document 3.2 above. For a detailed guide see R. G. Mulgan, (1978). *Aristotle's Political Theory: An Introduction for Students of Political Theory*. Oxford: OUP.

This philosophical concern with the role of the citizen is all very well but what relevance does it have to the real world? The answer is that such ideas do percolate down to the level of the ordinary citizen and form part of his or her personal values. That this is so can be shown, for example, by reporting on some research that has been done into the impact of civics courses in America. As part of this research, a representative sample of American students were asked how they would define the role of a citizen. In their answers the two attributes repeatedly mentioned were loyalty to their country and participation in its affairs. Interestingly, it was found that black students emphasized loyalty more than participation and this increased with attendance at civics courses and also according to the extent of education their parents had experienced. This correlation was explained as being due to the difficulties experienced by black people in participating in American politics and to the need for a sense of belonging among American blacks.

The values that citizens hold about their role in the political system, as well as other aspects of their political behaviour, form part of what is called 'political culture'. As Howard Elcock has put it: 'the type of culture existing in society will determine the part the citizens play, and expect to play in its affairs' (Elcock 1976, p. 59). By political culture we mean orientations towards politics generally and the political system in particular; orientations which consist of attitudes, values, beliefs, images, and symbols. Political cultures are transmitted within societies through a process of political socialization (see Concept Box 3.2).

Concept Box 3.2   Political Socialization

. . . the immediate source of a culture or subculture is the political socialization process by which cultures are maintained modified, or changed. By this term we refer to the lifelong inculcation and absorption of beliefs, values, and behavioural norms which begins in the cradle and ends in the grave.

The process is carried on by various socialization agents common to most societies, but different in their specific nature and impact. The first and generally most powerful agent is the family circle, the nuclear family in some societies, the extended in others. Generally the most durable values, norms, and political orientations are acquired through exposure to attitudes and beliefs prevailing within the family—to include even political party preferences . . . The beliefs and values acquired from the family are subsequently reinforced, modified, or in some cases changed by subsequent socialization experiences. The educational system seems to be second in importance, not only in terms of the content of educational programmes and the impact of teachers, but sometimes more by the influence of student peer groups. Then follow influences resulting from employment experiences, subsequent peer group influences emanating from people one associates with through life, mass media, and experiences resulting from direct contact with the political system—satisfaction, dissatisfactions, and frustrations. Major traumatic events experienced by a society—war, revolution, depression—may have a significant impact in so far as they are relayed to individuals through the various socialization agents. (Kolb 1978, p. 106)

From a normative perspective we have therefore concluded that there are two requirements of the citizen—to be obedient to the state and to participate in its affairs. These two roles have been considered conceptually from a philosophical angle and have been shown to have percolated down by a process of socialization to become part of the political culture of ordinary citizens. Our original question, however, asked what the role of citizens should be in 'a liberal democracy'. The following section seeks to clarify what is meant by this concept. We begin with a general statement on the wider concept of democracy and then go on to elucidate various alternative formulations of it, one of which will be that of *liberal* democracy.

Concept Box 3.3 Democracy

Like so many of the social science concepts examined in this book, the concept of democracy has a multitude of meanings and no one is universally acceptable. This reflects the fact that the concept is regarded with near universal approval since almost all states would claim that they are democracies. Adding to the confusion is the fact that the meaning of the word has changed through history: in earlier times it was often identified with the notion of tyrannical majority rule by the masses in their own self-interest.

Although there is no one generally acceptable definition of

democracy there is one that is very widely known. It is the famous formulation by Abraham Lincoln of 'government of the people, by the people, for the people.' This definition, like the concept itself, is so general and inexact that social scientists now commonly preface the word 'democracy' by a number of distinguishing terms. Liberal Democracy, for example, can be distinguished from Socialist Democracy; and within Liberal Democracy the further distinctions can be made of Representative and Participatory Democracy. Some of these distinctions are considered in the text. In all the variants, however, the central idea is that the people as a whole hold political power and have the right to make decisions.

The term Liberal Democracy can best be understood first of all as descriptive of states containing certain political characteristics. The following are the characteristics of Liberal Democracies that A. R. Ball has chosen to highlight in his book *Modern Politics and Government*. Of these characteristics, we can say that the first three seek to emphasize the democratic nature of such states and the final four characteristics emphasize the particular notion of democracy derived from liberal political ideas in the nineteenth century.

(1) There is more than one political party competing for power.
(2) Entry and recruitment to positions of political power are relatively open.
(3) There are periodic elections based on universal franchise.
(4) Competition for power is open not secretive, and is based on established and accepted forms of procedure.
(5) Pressure groups are able freely to operate to influence government decisions.
(6) Civil liberties, such as freedom of speech, religion, freedom from arbitary arrest, are recognized and protected within the political system.
(7) There is some form of separation of powers, i.e. a representative assembly has some form of control over the executive and the judiciary is independent of both executive and legislature.

Countries that conform, at least in part, to these characteristics are those of North America, Western Europe, Japan, and Australia. To most of the people of these countries it would be anathema to consider the states of Eastern Europe and China as democracies and they are often classified alternatively as 'totalitarian' states. But members of these other states would claim that their countries are the only true democracies. This view derives from a different, perhaps more long-lived, notion of democracy—what we can refer to here as Socialist Democracy. The major characteristic of this form of democracy has been defined by Holden as follows:

the 'decisions' of the people are incorporated in a single will. The will of the people is expressed (and perhaps ascertained) by a single party and is executed by the government under the close guidance of the party. Limitations on the government are not necessary, and would indeed be regarded as undemocratic since it would constitute a limitation of the will of the people. (Holden 1974, p. 35)

Liberal Democracy can therefore be understood as a form of political system that possesses certain liberal and democratic characteristics that distinguish it from Socialist Democracy which claims adherence to a different strand of democratic tradition and possesses alternative characteristics. Further understanding of the concept of Liberal Democracy can be gained by distinguishing two separate strands within it—Representative and Participatory Democracy. Each of these strands gives a somewhat different emphasis on the form that the participative role of citizens should take. Representative Democracy, as we shall see, emphasizes taking part in elections, and Participatory Democracy emphasizes a much broader range of action.

Representative Democracy is a variant of liberal democracy which stresses the primary importance of periodic popular elections between competing candidates for political office. The notion of Representative Democracy also contains a distinctive view on the relationship between the electorate and those elected by them. This relationship is not seen as a chain of command by which those who are elected become the instructed 'delegates' of the people who elected them. Instead those who are elected—now properly termed 'representatives'—take into account the interests and opinions of the electors but retain the right to use their own judgement as to how they should be acted upon when deciding on public affairs. Thus in Britain a majority of MPs vote against capital punishment even though opinion polls make it clear that most British citizens believe that some murderers should be executed. Elected representatives are of course seen as eventually answerable for their actions and judgements at a subsequent election.

To those who adhere to the more representative view of liberal democracy, the major expectations with regard to participation are heavily influenced by the writings of one of the founding fathers of modern liberal democratic theory—John Stuart Mill.

Profile 3.2 John Stuart Mill (1806–1873)

His life

John Stuart Mill was born is 1806. His father, James Mill, was a close friend of Jeremy Bentham and together they developed the school of political philosophy known as Utilitarianism which was of major importance throughout the nineteenth century. These two men took responsibility for the young boy's schooling and by all accounts he had a remarkable education. By the age of 4 he was learning Greek, and four years later he was studying arithmetic and Latin. In his early teens he mastered logic and political economy. All this required exclusion from play and contact with other children, a matter which Mill seems subsequently to have regretted. 'I never was a boy; never played at cricket; it is better to let Nature have her way', he once said. At the age of 17 he gained employment in India House as a clerk and some thirty-five years later he became Chief Examiner in the East India Company.

His intellectual training and education, based on the principles of utilitarianism, were tempered as a result of a severe depression which he experienced in 1826. He explains his recovery in his *Autobiography* as due to the discovery of the poetry of Wordsworth. The whole experience was to give him much deeper insights into the nature of happiness and human relationships. It was soon after this that he met Harriet Taylor who he eventually married in 1851 after the death of her husband. Their marriage, though happy, was overshadowed by Harriet's ill health and she died in 1858.

Mill's job allowed him considerable freedom to write and as well as publishing books he wrote widely in journals and for a time was the owner and director of the influential *London and Westminster Review*. When the East India Company was wound up in 1858 he gave himself full time to his writing but between 1865 and 1868 he sat in the House of Commons as MP for Westminster. During this short parliamentary career he concerned himself with electoral reform and the ever-present Irish question. After his defeat in the 1868 General Election he went to live with his stepdaughter, Helen Taylor, in France, and rarely returned to England. He died of a local fever in May 1873 and was buried next to his wife in Avignon.

His works

Mill's writings span the whole breadth of his life. As well as his considerable output of articles for journals and reviews, he published many books. Of these books the ones most frequently referred to today are: A *System of Logic* (1843), *On Liberty* (1859), *Considerations on Representative Government* (1861), *Utilitarianism* (1863), and *Three Essays on Religion* (1874). These works, taken as a whole, represent Mill's attempt to break away from the strict deductive analysis of utilitarianism as taught to him by his father and Bentham. From this perspective all aspects of society could be understood and ordered according to the fundamental principle that by nature people seek pleasure and avoid pain. Mill's *Logic* attempts to offer a more expansive method for analysing society taking into account not just a priori principles but also the lessons of history, empirical facts, and a greater role for creative thought (especially by the intellectual élite). In *On Liberty* Mill establishes freedom and individuality as equally important ends to that of pleasure but adds that he is not advocating unfettered freedom: 'The only freedom which deserves the name is that of pursuing our own good in our own way, so long as we do not attempt to deprive others of theirs, or impede their efforts to obtain it.' *Utilitarianism* returns to the concept of pleasure but rejects the view that all pleasures are equal by distinguishing as superior pleasures those that are lasting and socially valuable. Among these higher pleasures that need to be elevated and improved by society are those of duty, sacrifice, truth, beauty, the arts, and the public good. Mill's views on the political system are expounded upon in *Representative Government* which contains a classic portrayal of how a liberal democracy should be organized in terms of elections, assemblies, and the structure of government, and throughout Mill is concerned with the protection of minorities, although of these he particularly emphasized the intellectual élite whose voice he considered should be given greater weight than that of others. In his *Three Essays on Religion* Mill returns to his more developed concept of happiness and proposes that its highest elements, and especially that of a concern for the general good of others, should be elevated to a religion to replace those based upon the notion of the supernatural.

His importance

It is largely as a political philosopher addressing issues like liberty and representative government that Mill is most remembered. But he had a profound effect on the emerging social sciences at the end of the nineteenth century in the matter of methodology and he made an important contribution to the classical economics of the time. He also offered a more tempered and less mechanistic view of human nature. In this sense it could be argued that his importance lies in the fact that ethically he instilled into capitalist societies a concern for the common good against that of individual greed, and politically he provided guidelines for accommodating the growing strength of the working classes.

Writing in the second half of the nineteenth century, Mill emphasized the crucial importance of the vote as a means of ensuring democracy. He did not see the possession of a vote as a universal right, but rather argued that citizens should satisfy certain requirements in order to be given the vote: namely, the ability to read, write, and to have some skill in arithmetic. Mill went so far as to advocate that either the uneducated should be denied a vote, or the educated should be given more than one vote. As an alternative to some kind of educational test, Mill suggested that a person's occupation could be taken as a measure of a person's ability and experience, and hence fitness to vote. As well as possessing these qualifications, Mill would have further required the citizen to be informed about social life and to be knowledgeable about government and the law.

The franchise is no longer restricted to those with certain education, occupation, or property characteristics—it is now virtually universal—but we retain the view that the primary requirement of the liberal democratic citizen as far as participation is concerned is to vote and to be informed about political affairs.

The other form of Liberal Democracy is what we are calling Participatory Democracy. Elections, which are given primacy in the variant of Representative Democracy, are seen by the advocates of Participatory Democracy as too blunt and restricted an instrument for indicating by themselves the preferences of the people to their governments. Instead, Participatory Democracy views democracy in broader terms as a state of affairs in which citizens are more fully involved in the organization and regulation of their lives. From the standpoint of Participatory Democracy, then, the citizen might be expected to be involved in a much wider range of political activities than just voting and one way to present these additional forms of participation is by a ladder as shown in Document 3.4.

Document 3.4 The Ladder of Participation

Holder of Political Office

Candidate for Political Office

Active Member of Group and/or Party

Member of a Political Party

Member of a Pressure Group

Attender of Public Meetings, Demonstrations, Etc.

Contacting Public Official

Involved in Political Discussions

Informed About/Interested in Political Affairs

Voter

We are now in a position to summarize our normative response to the question of the role of citizens in a liberal democracy. That role is seen as the twofold one of obedience to the state and participation in its affairs. The extent of participation required of the citizen depends upon which variant of Liberal Democracy is being considered. Representative Democracy largely restricts the participative role to voting and being informed about political affairs. Participatory Democracy, as its name implies, requires far more from citizens by way of participation such as attending political meetings and joining groups and parties.

Empirical Issues

It is the ladder of participation that provides the basis for the

Table 3.1. Electoral Turnout, Various Nations

Nation	Name of Legislature	Election Year	Turnout (%)	Average Turnout 1960–78 (%)
Australia[1]	House of Representatives	—		95
Ireland	Dail	1983	63.5	75
New Zealand	House of Representatives	1984	85.9	88
Sweden	Riksdag	1982	91.5	88
UK	House of Commons	1983	73	75
USA[2]	House of Representatives	1980	47.4	58.9
USA[3]	House of Representatives	1982	38.1	41.8
FRG	Bundestag	1983	89.1	89

[1] Compulsory voting introduced in 1924.
[2] Year when Presidential election coincides with election to House of Representatives.
[3] Mid-term of President's office. Election to House of Representatives.

other—empirical—response to the original question about the role of citizens in liberal democracies. Here we are concerned with what the actual role of the citizen is in practice. A considerable amount of empirical evidence exists on the extent and nature of participation in political systems. Using the ladder of participation we can consider the evidence on the proportion of citizens in different countries that are involved on some of the rungs of the ladder ranging from voting to holding political office.

The bottom rung of our ladder of participation is voting, so we need to ask what proportion of citizens perform this basic requirement of liberal democracies. The most straightforward measure of this is electoral turnout and figures on this are calculated by showing those who actually vote as a percentage of the electorate. Table 3.1 compares electoral turnout for a number of different states and shows that there is considerable variation between them.

From the evidence presented in Table 3.1 we can see that Australia appears to have the greatest extent of voter participation, and this is achieved because voting is legally compulsory in that country. West Germany, New Zealand, and Sweden achieve almost as high a level, but without legal compulsion. The UK figures are low by comparison, but are still much higher than in the USA. In part, the low turnout in the USA can be explained by the complex procedures for registering as an elector.

Calculating the electoral turnout is reasonably simple because the basic data are publicly available. In order to discover rates of participation (and who it is participates) on the higher rungs of the ladder, more complex methods are required. Central to these methods is the collection of information through the use of social surveys. What these are and some of the issues surrounding them are examined in Method Box 3.1.

Method Box 3.1 Social Surveys

A social survey is a method which is widely used in social science to gather information by means of interviews and/or questionnaires with a carefully selected number of respondents. There has been a considerable increase in their use since the early 1950s. They are almost the only way of gathering certain information—especially that concerning the attitudes and perceptions of individuals, and also behaviour that cannot be directly observed. An obvious example here is voting behaviour since voting takes place in private. We cannot directly observe such behaviour, but through surveys we have gained a deep understanding of the effect of social background, the views and attitudes of electors, and other factors influencing voting.

The use of social surveys involves a number of stages from the initial formulation of the subject to be researched through to reporting on the processed data. Particularly important to an understanding of the technique are the stages of sampling, devising the interviews, and undertaking field-work.

Since it is not possible to question everyone, *sampling* is concerned with how many people should be questioned, and how they should be chosen. In terms of the number to be sampled this depends upon the size and characteristics of the total relevant 'population'. In terms of who are to be surveyed a variety of methods are available, of which 'quota' and 'random' samples are the most well known. Quota samples are used where certain key characteristics like sex or class are essential to the analysis and interviewers are instructed to find and question given numbers of those possessing such characteristics proportionate to their distribution in the 'population'. Random samples, on the other hand, are based upon theories of probability in that the sample to be interviewed is selected by a process that not only gives each element in the population an equal chance of being included in the sample, but also makes the selection of every possible combination of the desired number of cases equally likely. A simple example would be to take every tenth name on electoral registers of the area to be covered. Usually some division of the 'population' by *stratum* such as region or locality (different kinds of constituencies, for example) is first made from which random samples are then taken.

In devising the interviews to be used in the survey, the researcher has a choice between conducting them face to face, by post, or by telephone. Each has its relative advantages and disadvantages and choice will be determined by the nature of the project and the resources available. All, however, require some form of questionnaire and great care has to be taken with the wording, language, and form of the questions. One important distinction is between 'open-ended' questions, where respondents can answer freely, and 'closed-ended' questions, where answers have to be chosen from given responses.

In undertaking the field-work pre-testing the questionnaire is often an essential preliminary to make sure that unforeseen problems can be dealt with. Where a questionnaire is administered other than by post, interviewers need to be trained. The key to successful field-work is to achieve a high response rate.

All of these issues and problems in social surveying are essentially concerned with the same end—to avoid bias (or distortion) in the collection of evidence. Thus, for example, the sample interviewed must be representative, leading questions avoided, and interviewers need to be careful not to influence respondents.

There is a vast body of social survey evidence on the extent of participation by citizens at the various levels of political activity. It is only possible to refer to a very small part of all of the available evidence in our present consideration of the actual role that citizens play in liberal democracies. Some individual findings will be mentioned, but what follows is largely based on two useful summaries of the evidence for a limited number of countries.

The first summary of the extent of citizen participation at different levels of political activity is by Richard Rose (1980) who has gathered together survey findings on the involvement of citizens in British politics in the form of a table which is reproduced in an amended form as Table 3.2.

The second summary of survey evidence on participation comes from a major work on this subject by S. Verba and N. H. Nie. Table 3.3 is a much simplified version of a table taken from their book and covers other Western liberal democracies of the USA and the

Table 3.2. Involvement in British Politics

Level	Estimated Number of People	Estimated % of Electorate
Voters, General Election 1983	30,700,000	73
Organization members	24,000,000	61
Voters, Local Elections	17,000,000	42
Knows name of Council Chairman/Mayor	11,500,000	28
Great deal of interest in politics	8,000,000	19
Ever contacted local councillor	6,800,000	17
Official post in organization	5,500,000	14
Political activist	2,800,000	7
Attended protests or demonstrations	2,500,000	6
Individual party members	2,000,000	5
MP, Senior Civil Servant, or Councillor	25,700	0.06

Source: Based on Rose 1980, Table VI.1 (p. 173) and Table VI.2 (p. 178).

Netherlands, together with data from India, Japan, and Nigeria.

Selected data on political participation by means of taking part in elections have already been considered but for many voters this may be no more than a fairly ritualized activity. Participation at higher levels requires rather more from the citizen in terms of effort and

Table 3.3. Political Participation in Five Countries

Activity	India	Japan	Netherlands	Nigeria	USA
Ever worked for a political party	25	25	—	—	26
Attended political meeting/rally	14	50	9	—	19
Member of a political club or organization	6	4	13	—	8
Active member of organization engaged in solving community problem	7	11	15	28	32
Worked through group on community problem	18	51	16	32	30
Helped form group to deal with a community problem	5	5	24	24	14
Contacted local official on social issue	4	11	7	2	14
Contacted local offical on personal matter	12	7	38	2	7

Per cent who say 'yes' or perform act regularly

Source: Based on Verba et al. 1978, pp. 58–9.

Table 3.4. Interest in Politics in the United
Kingdom (%)

Level of Interest	1962[1]	1969[2]
Very interested	15	8
Interested	37	34
Not very interested	33	41
Not interested	15	17

[1] Rush and Althoff 1971.
[2] National Opinion Poll 1969.

knowledge of the system. The rewards for increased political involvement, however, is the likelihood of having a greater impact on affairs. A minimal starting-point for political involvement beyond that of voting is that individuals have some interest in the politics of their country. Most surveys show that a significant proportion of the population do not even reach this rung of the ladder. Table 3.4 gives the results of two British surveys for 1962 and 1969 and they can be contrasted with the figure of 19 per cent of the electorate having a great deal of interest given in Table 3.2, drawn from a 1974 survey. Clearly the figures fluctuate from year to year and perhaps reflect the political scene at the time of the survey. But all the British surveys indicate that close to one-half of the electorate have little interest in politics and thus, it might be argued, are unlikely to be present on the higher rungs of the political ladder. They have been referred to as the political lumpenproletariat.

Figures on contacting public officials and attending public meetings and demonstrations can be gleaned from Tables 3.2 and 3.3 and some interesting contrasts can be detected. Apart from the higher figures for Japan, however, it appears that we are now down to less than one-fifth of the electorate.

Pressure group membership, both passive and active, is very difficult to measure since the term pressure group is used differently in the various pieces of research. Verba and Nie's figures refer to 'political clubs or organizations'. Other data refer to 'voluntary organizations'. Interest in this rung is also often restricted to the local political level. The best estimate that can be given of pressure group membership for Britain is that around 30 per cent of the electorate belong to groups apart from parties which attempt to influence the political process, and only about half this number are active within them.

Party membership can be more accurately counted but in the British context a distinction has to be made between Labour Party members who join by not contracting out when they join an affiliated trade union and those who join as individuals. Rose estimated that only 5 per cent of the British electorate count as individual party members. This compares with around 3 per cent of the West German electorate, 2½ per cent in France and 4 per cent in the USA.

At the summit of the ladder, Rose suggests that only 25,700 people can be counted as holders of political office and he includes senior Civil Servants in this category. They represent a mere 0.06 per cent of the electorate.

Clearly then, apart from voting, political participation is a minority pursuit among the citizens of liberal democracies. Also of importance is the fact that the minority who do participate are not socially representative of citizens as a whole. This point has been made most forcefully by the writers from whom we derived Table 3.3:

In no society is the activist portion of the population a representative sample of the population as a whole. In most societies that have been studied and for most kinds of political activity, a person is more likely to be politically active if he is male, middle-aged, relatively wealthy, well-educated, and, perhaps, from the dominant ethnic, religious or racial groups. (Nie and Verba 1975, p. 38)

In support of Nie and Verba's general contention about the social unrepresentativeness of those who are active political participants, we can examine some of the many research findings on this matter. Going back to the issue of interest in politics, the 1962 survey by Rush and Althoff showed the following social variations between those uninterested in politics: 40 per cent of men compared to 57 per cent of women and only 31 per cent of middle-class respondents compared to 56 per cent of working-class respondents were reported to be so inclined. A survey of voluntary organization membership in the UK, the USA, and West Germany gives some indication of the variations for those participating in group activities. In all three countries, two-thirds of men were found to be members of voluntary organizations whereas the proportion of women was found to be much lower (47 per cent in the USA, 30 per cent in the UK, and only 24 per cent in West Germany). The research also illustrated the

Table 3.5. Background of British MPs (1983)

	Conservative	Labour	Alliance
Number elected	397	209	23
Women (%)	3	5	0
Median age	47	51	44
EDUCATION (%)			
Public school	70	14	52
University	71	53	65
OCCUPATION (%)			
Professions	45	42	61
Business	36	9	4
Manual workers	1	33	0
Miscellaneous	19	16	35

importance of the variable of education. Around 40 per cent of those who have only received an elementary level of education appear to join voluntary organizations while for those who have experienced higher education the figures are much higher (80 per cent in the USA, 92 per cent in the UK, and 62 per cent in West Germany). These variations in the social representativeness of voluntary group members become even more pronounced when leadership positions in such groups are considered.

If we turn to the final rung of the ladder—that of holding political office—we can see that the social unrepresentativeness becomes yet further pronounced. Table 3.5 looks at differences in the backgrounds of MPs elected to the British House of Commons in 1983. It quite clearly shows that despite some significant differences between the parties, the House of Commons is far from being a social microcosm of the electorate.

In seeking an understanding of the extent and distribution of political participation in liberal democracies we can turn to the alternative social science perspectives that were introduced in chapter 1.

From an individualist perspective, the differences between those who participate and those who do not would be accounted for in terms of personality and ability. The individualist perspective might also take up the theme of the assumed rationality of individuals and argue that different rates of participation can be explained by the notion of the opportunity cost of participation, i.e. the value of the alternative uses to which resources (such as time and money) could be put by the individual, estimating the benefit that might accrue from participation compared to some other form of action. From this standpoint, one writer has concluded:

> . . . not many of the highly educated and well-to-do in affluent Western countries ordinarily put much time into politics. Neither do many of the poor, because they either lack motivation (having suffered too much, knowing too little, and being too busy keeping body and soul together) or lack rewards. . . . And even the poor take opportunity costs into account: a poor person might prefer watching television or visiting a bar to talking politics—particularly if politics in the past had not produced any early and visible improvements.
>
> . . . Thus, the professional people on the one hand and the poor on the other are underrepresented in the day-to-day political process in many Western democracies, whereas many members of the lower middle-class, particularly long-time residents of local communities, choose routine politics as one of their favourite indoor games. (Deutsch 1974, pp. 58–9)

From a pluralist perspective would come the view that differences between countries with regard to the extent of participation can be accounted for by differing attitudes towards participation within a country's political culture, different levels of socio-economic development, and the extent of group differentiation and organization. The pluralist might also support the introduction of more mechanisms like referendums and public meetings to encourage greater participation. They might also favour more open access to information and more encouragement for political participation by the education system.

To those of an élitist persuasion the evidence on participation would be quoted to support their general view that there will always be leaders and the led, and that much of the distinction can be explained in terms of differing psychological predispositions.

The Marxist perspective would also quote the findings to support their position that in a capitalist society participation is largely restricted to those from the capitalist class, or those closely associated by birth, education, and occupation with it. The apparent encouragement of participation is seen as no more than another device to legitimize what is basically class rule. It is 'apparent encouragement' because the evidence shows that the capitalist state historically has strongly resisted attempts by ordinary citizens to get involved in the affairs of the state.

Conclusions

Our general question was to ask what role citizens should play in a liberal democracy. From a normative stance we distinguished the twofold roles of obedience to the state and participation in its affairs. The extent of participation required of the citizen was different for the representative and participatory variants of liberal democratic theory. From an empirical stance, citizens appear to have fulfilled the requirements of representative democracy but have not done so either in significant numbers or evenly throughout society in terms of the more demanding requirements of participatory democracy. Explanations for the failure of citizens to fulfil the role set for them by participatory democracy vary according to the alternative social science perspectives that exist.

It finally remains to clarify how the different social science disciplines fit into the above analysis. The discipline of law is of relevance to an understanding of the key term of 'citizen' but the bulk of analysis is derived from political science and in particular three of its sub-branches: those of political theory, comparative politics, and political sociology. Political theory has addressed itself to the normative consideration of what the role of the citizen ought to be and two of its founding fathers—Aristotle and John Stuart Mill—have been referred to together with the central political concept of democracy. Comparative politics, as the name implies, is particularly concerned to compare and contrast the political systems of different countries. The findings of Nie and Verba fit closely to this branch of political science. Political sociology, on the other hand, exists at the interface between political science and sociology. This interface contains the area of study which looks at the impact of social phenomena like class and the educational system on political matters like voting and party membership. A key concept in political sociology is that of socialization and we shall see in the next chapter that it is a concept that has been most fully developed within the discipline of sociology.

References

Aristotle. *The Politics*, trans. T. A. Sinclair. (1962). Harmondsworth: Penguin.

Ball, A. R. (1983). *Modern Politics and Government* 3rd edn. London: Macmillan.

Brogan, D. W. (1960). *Citizenship Today*. NC: University of North Carolina Press.

Deutsch, K. W. (1974). *Politics and Government*. London: Houghton Mifflin.

Elcock, H. (1976). *Political Behaviour*. London: Metheun.

Finer, S. E. (1979). *Five Constitutions*. Harmondsworth: Penguin.

Gould, J., and W. L. Kolb (eds.) (1964). *A Dictionary of the Social Sciences*. London: Tavistock.

Holden, B. (1974). *The Nature of Democracy*. London: Nelson.

Kolb, E. J. (1978). *A Framework for Political Analysis*. Engelwood Cliffs: Prentice Hall.

Mulgan, R. G. (1978). *Aristotle's Political Theory: An Introduction for Students of Political Theory*. Oxford: OUP.

Nie, N. H., and Verba S. (1975). In F. I. Greenstein (ed.) (1975). *Handbook of Political Sciences*. Reading, Mass.: Addison-Wesley.

Rose, R. (1980). *Politics in England Today. An Interpretation For the 1980s*. London: Faber and Faber.

Rush, M., and Althoff P. (1971). *An Introduction to Political Sociology*. London: Nelson.

Verba, S. *et al.* (1978). *Participation and Political Equality: A Seven Nation Comparison*. Cambridge: CUP.

4 The Changing Family

Social scientists study people in society. If, somewhere in the Universe, there existed a person who had never been in contact with any other human, social scientists would be fascinated because this would enable them to estimate the importance of human interaction. There have been one or two cases of 'wolf children'—children deserted by their parents and taken care of by animals. Such children cannot talk and their behaviour is animal-like; for example, they tend to crawl rather than walk. These cases of wolf children are, of course, extremely rare but there are several examples of children being brought up in isolation; for example, illegitimate children whose mothers fear the shame which may occur in some societies and so keep the birth secret. Such children may live alone in an attic, be fed but not spoken to, kept alive but not cared for. Such children also behave somewhat like wolf children.

These examples suggest that what makes people human is 'society', that is meeting and interacting with other people. Our ideas, beliefs, abilities, and personalities are not fixed at birth but are substantially affected by the people around us, and probably the most important influence on our lives is our family. The family provides a base from which we can journey out into the world. It affects the way we think and act and the kind of people we become. We spend a large part of our waking lives in families and its effect is incalculable. It is, therefore, not surprising that scientists, especially sociologists, have spent much time studying families.

This chapter tries to study *how* social scientists have studied the family, using as a focus the question 'Is the family changing?'. This is an important question because, if the family as an institution changes, people in the next generation will grow up in a changed environment, becoming different kinds of people from their parents.

Everybody knows what we mean when we talk about 'the family' yet like so many key concepts in social science it is difficult to define precisely. In everyday life we can make do with vague understandings, but social scientists, just as much as scientists studying the physical world, need precision. This is often difficult to achieve for everyday social phenomena. For example, which of the following are families:

(a) a person living on his or her own in his or her own house;
(b) two unrelated students sharing a flat;
(c) a group of nuns living in the same house;
(d) a man and woman living together in the same house but not married;
(e) a married couple whose children have left home;
(f) a elderly couple living with the wife's widowed mother;
(g) a unmarried mother living with her child; and
(h) a wife with a husband away at sea or in prison?

There is clearly no agreed definition of family and there is room for genuine disagreement over its meaning. Murdock (1949) defined the family as a 'social group characterised by common residence, economic cooperation and reproduction. It includes adults of both sexes, at least two of whom maintain a socially approved sexual relationship, and one or more children born or adopted of the socially cohabiting adults.'

What Murdock is defining here is not generally accepted as a definition of a family because it is much too restrictive. He would not include as families any of the types listed above. A rather broader definition is given by Burgess and Locke (1953): 'The family is a group of persons united by ties of marriage, blood or adoption; constituting a simple household interacting and intercommunicating with each other in their respective social role of husband and wife, mother and father, brother and sister; creating a common culture.' (The authors are using the word 'culture' in its sociological sense referring to the whole way of life of a group and not limiting it to 'high culture' such as music and literature.) This definition is broader than that of Murdock and it stresses why the family is of interest to sociologists, because the people interact with each other to produce shared values and opinions, even though these are sometimes rejected by some members of the family. Thus the children of people with strong religious beliefs will usually accept these beliefs, but a few will be apathetic and some will reject religion entirely.

This question of definition is important because if there is no agreement on what is meant by 'family' it is difficult to analyse its role in society. For example, how can we answer even a basic question such as 'is the average size of the family falling?' if we cannot say precisely what we mean by family? Social science requires precise use of words.

Because the family is such an important social institution it arouses strong feelings. When James Callaghan was Prime Minister of Great Britain he said, 'The over-riding social concern is to preserve and enhance the influence of the family as a whole: an influence which is beneficial in every way' (quoted in Nobbs, 1983, p. 139). Contrast this with the views of Sir Edmund Leach (1968) in his Reith Lectures: 'Far from being the basis of a good society the family with its narrow privacy and tawdry secrets is the source of all our discontents.'

Method Box 4.1 Objectivity and Subjectivity in Social Science

Differences in opinion about the worth of the family are specific examples of a general problem in social science: that of subjectivity. In astronomy, calculating the distance of a star from the Earth is a technical matter, it doesn't involve values, attitudes, or lifestyles. In social science one basic difficulty is that the subjective beliefs of the researchers may affect their findings. *The facts do not speak for themselves.* They are not impartial. They have to be interpreted. If two people supporting opposite teams go to a football match what they see will be influenced by their partisan views. A defender goes for the ball, the attacking forward falls; is it a foul? The facts of the incident do not vary, but spectators will view the incident very differently. So it is in social science. Those who believe that the family is a most valuable social institution will see family quarrels as merely an interruption in a strong continuing relationship. Those who question the value of the family will see them as evidence of the inevitable conflicts which arise in a restricting institution. The problem of subjectivity is not limited to social scientists studying the family, for it affects huge areas of research and study. Social class, race, religion, poverty, unemployment, elections—all these create strong feelings in social scientists as they do in the rest of the population, and the perceptions of social scientists will be influenced by their beliefs; thus, even when trying to be objective, what is seen and reported will inevitably be affected by preconceived opinions. This has implications for those reading social science books. It is relatively easy to see bias in the opinions of those expressing very different opinions from ours; what is less easy is to discern bias in those writers whose views reflect our own. The discriminating reader should always try to ascertain the writer's beliefs in order to read critically, making allowance for the values of the writer.

Forms of the Family

To many of us the family seems to be a natural institution existing throughout the world and deep into the past. However, many of the functions carried out by the family, such as the care of children, are sometimes undertaken outside the family. In Israel the traditional kibbutz is a collective settlement, usually concerned with cultivating the land and where most property is held in common and decisions are taken collectively. The children are often brought up in a children's house by trained personnel and parents have relatively little contact with their children, although the practice varies between communes. In the U S A in the nineteenth century a number of 'Utopian' communities were set up where the community as a whole was responsible for child care. More recently, communes have been established in a number of countries which attempt to break down family ties so that people can live together with the emphasis on group life.

These examples are relatively rare: the family could claim to be the most widespread human institution. However, the structure and organization of the family does vary considerably. One way of analysing family structure is to consider the number of wives or husbands a person may be married to at any one time. In most Western societies *monogamy* exists and a person is limited to one marriage partner at a time. This kind of marriage is most common in the developed countries where the Christian influence has been important. However, Murdock (1949) studied 238 societies and found that only 43 of these were monogamous, though these included most of the main centres of population. The alternative to monogamy is *polygamy* where a person can be married to several people at the same time. In a few rare cases this takes the form of *polyandry* where a woman can have more than one husband at the same time. There are examples of this in the Himalayan foothills. More common is *polygyny* where a man can have two or more wives at the same time. This is common in Islamic countries and in many parts of Africa. Although polygyny is permitted in many societies, relatively few men can afford to marry more than one wife. In the first place there may not be a surplus of women, secondly, it is often expensive—in many African countries a man may have to pay a bride-price in the form of cattle and would need to be relatively wealthy to marry more than once. In some cases the second marriage is purely a formality. If a woman is left a widow it may be expected that she would 'marry' her husband's brother in order to have the support of the family. A marriage such as this may be more concerned with property, social position, and care of the elderly than with sex or the more personal aspects of a marriage.

Concept Box 4.1 Nuclear and Extended Families

The nuclear family is a single household unit comprising husband, wife, and children.

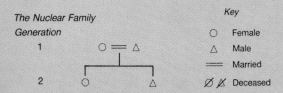

This is the typical type of family in industrial countries, though nuclear families have existed for centuries. Most people live in two nuclear families in their lifetime: firstly as children and secondly as parents. Exceptions to the nuclear family include people living on their own or single parent families.

In the extended family more than two generations live together so that grandparents are an integral part of the family.

The family may also be extended horizontally so that cousins, uncles, aunts are considered part of the family and may come and

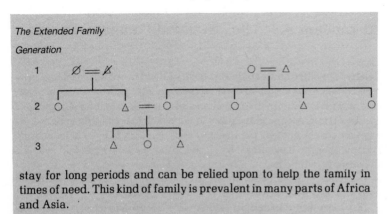

The Extended Family

Generation

stay for long periods and can be relied upon to help the family in times of need. This kind of family is prevalent in many parts of Africa and Asia.

In every society, when a marriage takes place a couple have to decide where to live. In most contemporary Western societies the couple try to set up a new home of their own, although they may be forced to live with relatives because they do not have enough money to form their own home. In other societies the pattern may be very different; the newly married couple may be expected to live with or near the bride's parents; or the expectation may be that that the woman will move and the couple will reside with the groom's parents.

The place of residence is often linked to the way in which people reckon their descent. In advanced industrial countries, for example, the wife takes on her husband's name and the children will also bear their father's name. Sometimes only sons can inherit the family estate or titles. Despite this formal position, in everyday life relationships may be closer to the wife's family as the proverb suggests: 'My son's a son till he takes him a wife, but my daughter's a daughter all of her life.' In some societies the link with the mother's family is more formal. For example, in the Ashanti of Ghana the husband lives with his mother and only occasionally visits his wife; the children are not his in the social sense but hers and belong to her lineage. Rules about who a person can or cannot marry are particularly important in tribal communities because marriage bonds help to preserve tribal unity.

Document 4.1 The Extended Family in Samoa

Relatives in other households also play a role in the children's lives. Any older relative has a right to demand personal service from younger relatives, a right to criticize their conduct and to interfere in their affairs. Thus a little girl may escape alone down to the beach to bathe only to be met by an older cousin who sets her washing or caring for a baby or to fetch some coconut to scrub the clothes. So closely is the daily life bound up with this universal servitude and so numerous are the acknowledged relationships in the name of which service can be exacted, that for the children an hour's escape from surveillance is almost impossible.

This loose but demanding relationship group has its compensations also. Within it a child of three can wander safely and come to no harm, can be sure of finding food and drink, a sheet to wrap herself up in for a nap, a kind hand to dry casual tears and bind up her wounds . . . Few children live continuously in one household, but are always testing out other possible residences. And this can be done under the guise of visits and with no suggestion of truancy . . .

A relative is regarded as someone upon whom one has a multitude of claims and to whom one owes a multitude of obligations. From a relative one may demand food, clothing, and shelter, or assistance in a feud. Refusal of such a demand brands one as stingy and lacking in human kindness, the virtue most esteemed among Samoans.

Source: Margaret Mead (1928). *Coming of Age in Samoa*.

Reasons for Variation in the Form of the Family

Social scientists are not interested in these variations just for the sake of listing the differences; what is important is to explain them. Because family patterns are so varied and so complex they are not completely understood.

The obvious explanation is that individuals choose freely what kind of family they will form. There is some substance in this argument. In any one society a wide variety of living patterns will be found. However, when people *think* they are making a free choice they are often influenced unconsciously by strong pressures from society. There are few people who are so isolated from society that they are uninfluenced by the prevailing social values. People fall in love and get married partly because such behaviour is expected. 'Romantic love' is not a natural phenomenon; it is a creation of social factors in particular societies.

An alternative explanation of variations in the form of the family focuses on economic factors. The extended family—at its best—can bring the strength of a large family to help individuals. If a mother is ill or dies there will be plenty of other relatives able and willing to look after the children. Similarly there are always young people able to take care of the elderly. In many areas of Africa it is very common for a bright boy to be supported financially by his extended family so that he can obtain an education and, in turn, he will then be expected to help others. If a member of the family needs capital to start or expand a business the family will put together its resources, not only of capital but also of labour.

Document 4.2 The Extended Family in Britain

Over at Southall, Mr. K. D. Patel, formerly a Ugandan Asian, runs three large garages and buys and sells others as a side-line. He came here in 1972 with the general exodus and got a job with the Heron garage group as a trainee manager; he had been in the same line of business on his own account back home. All Asians thrown out by Amin were allowed to bring out just £300 a head. That means in his family's case £1,500; plus another £1,200 owed him by a fellow exile.

His wages at Heron were at first £1,400 a year and out of this exiguous sum all he could afford was a flat with one-and-a-half rooms for all five of them; his two children and two wives. *Two* wives? Yes—a beaming smile—well, one was what we call here his common-law wife. And how had they all got on in a room-and-a-half? Very well—as always. Indeed the charming young lady who had received me at the pay desk was his second wife; the first worked at one of his other garages.

Today Mr. Patel lives in a mansion at Wembley with a garden that looks as if it was inspired by the Taj Mahal. Inside the house he has a swimming pool and a disco to cope with lavish entertaining. He is the Great Gatsby of Wembley.

How on earth had it all been done? Well, he explained modestly, he'd done well at Heron. In six months his salary had risen to £2,500 and soon after that he was one of their top managers, moving to garages where they had problems to be sorted out—what we call a troubleshooter. In his five years at Heron he learned a lot about the garage trade in Britain. When he decided to go it alone, there were family and friends to help with capital.

Source: Godfrey Smith 'The Patels of Britain', *Sunday Times*, 26 February 1984.

The extended family can also bring disadvantages. If one member of the family does well economically, less successful relations are liable to arrive for an extended stay to share in the benefits. If this occurs the incentives to innovate or save may be reduced and this is one reason why the extended family is less common in advanced industrial countries than it is in developing countries.

In poorer countries there seem to be correlations between the form taken by the family and the available food supplies. Thus the bushmen of the Kalahari live and travel in small family groups whilst in areas where agrarian or pastoral agriculture is practised the extended family is more common. Tribes such as the Masai who inhabit the grasslands of East Africa wander over large areas with their cattle; children and old people can perform useful services to the family and it is therefore more efficient to have a large family. Similarly, in areas depending on subsistence agriculture old people can cook and look after children leaving other adults time to work the soil or care for the old. The extended family provides a kind of social security for the old and sick in countries too poor for the state to provide pensions.

There are, of course, non-economic reasons for variation in family pattern. Where men are more likely to die—for example in wars—a 'surplus' of women will exist. If there are expectations that most adults should be married then it is not surprising to find that some men will have more than one wife. Similarly, the early Mormons in the U S A allowed polygyny. This made sense, for the Church had more women members than men and allowing men to have more than one wife reduced the problem (as it was then often seen) of unmarried women. It would also encourage a high birth rate among church members and so allow the church to grow.

There is no fully satisfactory answer to the question 'why do family forms differ?' because there are so many factors that could have an influence. One reason is that the form of the family varies because the functions of the family vary between societies.

The Functions of the Family

In order to be able to discuss the question 'Is the family changing?' we need to consider what it is that the family *does*; in other words to analyse the functions of the family.

Regulating sexual behaviour

Probably all societies throughout history have had some rules designed to regulate sexual behaviour. This is because sex has a powerful influence on people and can be a constructive or destructive force in society. The rules concerning permitted sexual behaviour vary widely. Where religious influence is strong, for example in Christian and Muslim countries, sexual intercourse should only take place between husband and wife and the marriage service makes plain that this is one of the main functions of marriage; 'It is better to marry than to burn', said St Paul.

The prohibition of sexual activity outside marriage may serve a useful social function. The family is an important social institution; sexual activity outside marriage can threaten the stability and continuance of the family. A rule which prohibits sexual activity outside marriage helps to maintain social stability. It is clear that rules restricting sexual behaviour are frequently broken though it is not clear whether sex outside marriage is an increasing a phenomenon as the media would suggest, or whether it has always been widespread. Our ignorance of this area of human life is very considerable, partly because people are reluctant to discuss their sexual behaviour. Social scientists can obtain data on a wide variety of social phenomena affecting the family—the number of births and marriages, the prevalence of divorce, the amount of family income, for example. However, data on sexual activity are not only very sparse but are of questionable value since people often lie about their sexual activities. A number of surveys have asked people 'How often do you have sexual intercourse?' The answers invariably suggest that men have intercourse much more frequently than women! Consequently the statistics are of little value and it is difficult to make comparisons of extramarital sex between societies or with the past.

If sexual activity outside marriage is increasing it may be due in part to the development of better methods of birth-control which make it possible to engage in sexual intercourse without the risk of pregnancy. If the absence of satisfactory contraceptive methods in the past caused people to abstain from extramarital sex then such sexual activity may be on the increase. However, explanations in terms of the changing technology of birth-control are too narrow. It is more important to ascertain why people are willing to ignore the 'rules' of society concerning sex. Large areas of sexual behaviour are not subject to the law but to the influence of informal sanctions such as gossip or family pressure. These sanctions may be weakened if the influence of the community becomes more remote as it may in large urban areas where work, family, and social activities may be widely separated. The evidence is uncertain. Sexual activity outside marriage may or may not be increasing. In any event, much pre-marital intercourse takes place between partners who intend to get married. The family may still play an important part in limiting sexual behaviour to married couples or those about to marry.

Reproduction

Reproduction is a fundamental function of the family in all societies. Indeed, depending on the precise definition of the family, we may not recognize that a family exists until a married couple has children. In considering the reproductive function of the family, social scientists are not so much concerned with biology as with social reproduction, in other words with the way in which social descent is legitimized. Marx and Engels saw this as one of the most important functions of the family in a capitalist society because the inheritance of property depended on proof of parenthood. This is particularly important in capitalism because political power derives from the possession of property in the form of capital. Consequently, inheritance is a matter of central concern to those who possess property. In medieval times similar concerns applied to those who owned land. Execution was the penalty for men engaging in sex with the Queen. Legitimacy of descent was the central concern so that it was necessary for everyone to be certain that the father of the Queen's children was the King. No such sanctions applied to the King's sexual behaviour and many monarchs have been notorious seducers. For the upper classes, property mattered more than chastity so they were often more concerned that there should be a male heir than that the legal father should actually be the biological father.

Table 4.1. Legitimate and Illegitimate Births

England and Wales

	1961	1971	1981	1985
No. of births	811,000	783,000	634,000	656,000
No. of legitimate births	763,000	717,000	554,000	530,000
No. of illegitimate births	48,000	66,000	81,000	126,000
Illegitimate as % of total births	6	8	13	19

Source: Social Trends, No. 15, HMSO London (1986), Table 2.20.

Of course reproduction occurs outside the family as Table 4.1 shows. As the Table makes clear the number and the proportion of illegitimate births is increasing, at least in England and Wales. This may be seen by some people as evidence that the family is losing its function of controlling reproduction. One reason for the increase may lie in changing attitudes towards illegitimacy. In the past unmarried mothers were subject to considerable social sanctions and their children may have suffered from discrimination. However, the stigma attached to illegitimacy has largely disappeared and this has made women more willing to bear children when unmarried, whereas in the past they may have sought marriage, even to men they did not particularly wish to wed.

In some cases the unmarried mother will keep the child and form what may be regarded as an incomplete nuclear family; in others the child will be adopted and brought up in a nuclear family, though one that is different from its procreative family. In a few rare cases, illegitimate children will be brought up by their fathers. Some children, though technically illegitimate, are raised by their parents, who live together as a family even though they are not married to each other.

Method Box 4.2 Use and Limitations of Statistics

Almost all science makes considerable use of statistics and statistical methods. Whereas physical scientists generate much of their data in the course of experiments this is less common in social science, though some disciplines, such as psychology, do make use of experiments. Most social scientists make considerable use of officially produced statistics. Modern governments collect an enormous amount of material and much of this is published. Such data cover a wide area of social activity, ranging literally from birth to death and, in most countries, are objective and impartial. Social scientists also make use of other statistics such as those collected by social surveys or by private individuals or groups such as firms. Whilst these data may be useful it is often not objective and may have to be treated with a good deal of caution.

Whatever the source, statistics are needed to test hypotheses, to build up arguments, to test evidence, to reject false statements— in other words, to enable social scientists to think and work scientifically.

Statistics may be misused. Sometimes they are used as a drunk uses a lamp-post, for support rather than illumination. The perils of poor statistics are wittily presented in a little book by Darrell Huff (1954), 'How to Lie with Statistics' Harmondsworth: Penguin a book on statistics which does not require the reader to make a single calculation.

There are many limitations on the use of statistics by social scientists. Frequently they do not measure precisely what is required. For example, statistics on divorce do not really measure family breakdown because many couples separate without divorcing. Sometimes statistics give only a partial view—statistics on the number of millionaires in a society tell us very little about the distribution of income or the opportunities for individual advancement. At a more technical level, it is possible to disagree about matters such as which are the more suitable statistical tests to apply to data or the extent to which a case is proved or disproved by statistical evidence.

There is additional evidence to suggest that the reproductive function of the family has fallen in importance. In many countries the size of the family has declined during the last century as couples decide to have fewer children. Whatever the reasons for this, the decline in family size is evidence of a desire on the part of couples to restrict the family's reproductive function.

Child-rearing and socialization

A young baby is helpless. It cannot feed or take care of itself. For several years children need the care of adults. Whilst some children are brought up in orphanages, children's homes, or by foster parents who provide a surrogate 'family', the family remains the prime protector and nurturer of children.

The function of the family in this area goes far beyond taking care of the physical needs of the child because the family is perhaps the prime agent in the socialization of the child. The concept of socialization was introduced in chapter 2 in the context of work, but it is probably even more important when discussing the family. This is because the child spends so much time interacting with the members of its family at a time in its life when its attitudes and values are unformed. Once formed, many of the child's beliefs will be relatively stable.

It is considerations such as these that have led some sociologists to argue that socialization is the most important function of the family. Talcott Parsons believed that the American family had largely transcended functions such as regulating sexual behaviour and controlling procreation and that its functions were now twofold. The first of these was the primary socialization of children. As the child grows it becomes more aware of others and begins to learn to adjust its behaviour to allow for other people so that social behaviour develops. Through the family the child gradually *internalizes* the culture of its particular society. In other words, many aspects of everyday life become part of the child so that it does not have to think what to do or how to behave. The child realizes the kind of behaviour which is appropriate to a particular situation—for example, that it should eat in a particular way, that it should treat parents differently from strangers, that it should cross the road in a certain way.

Profile 4.1 Talcott Parsons (1902–1979)

His life

Talcott Parsons was born in Colorado Springs in the U S A. His father was a Congregational minister and also a teacher of English who later became the President of a small college in Ohio. He grew up in a religious atmosphere and seems to have had a happy childhood.

At first Parsons wanted to be a biologist or doctor but whilst at Amherst College in Massachusetts he developed an interest in social science, particularly in an aspect of economics which tried to analyse economic institutions and processes in terms of their effects on the wider society. Because this area of economics was related to sociology, he developed an interest in the main sociological ideas of the day.

After leaving Amherst in 1924 a generous uncle agreed to finance Parsons to a year's study at the London School of Economics where he became interested in anthropology and came into contact with the functionalist perspective which he later developed. It was at the LSE that he met his wife Helen and this meeting led to a lifelong happy relationship. Whilst at the LSE he obtained an exchange fellowship to Heidelberg University in Germany where he came into close contact with the ideas of Weber who had lived there earlier. At Heidelberg he obtained a D. Phil. Degree and then return to America to take up a post at Amherst to teach economics. Later he moved to Harvard, at first teaching economics, but by 1931 he had switched to sociology.

During the Second World War Parsons worked for the U S government largely on economic-political issues relating to the post-war reconstruction of Germany. During this time his elder brother and both his parents died causing him great distress and this led him to undergo psychoanalysis. In 1942 Parsons was appointed the head of a new interdisciplinary Department of Social Relations at Harvard. He wrote prolifically both during and after the war so that he rose to a leading position in his profession and in 1949 was elected President of the American Sociological Association.

In the 1950s the U S A became violently anti-communist and many people, particularly in the film industry, lost their jobs because they were suspected of communist associations. Academics also lost their jobs and Parsons, despite his reputation as a conservative, was vigorous in defending those accused.

In 1953 he moved to Cambridge University for a year as a visiting professor and noted that in Britain, sociology had a lower status than other social sciences. On his return to the U S A he continued his academic work and gained a dominant position in American sociology. He was seriously ill in 1968 and retired from Harvard in 1973 though he continued to write and collaborated with a number of his ex-students in a wide variety of studies—on religion, death, medical sociology, the family, and psychoanalysis.

He died in 1979 whilst on a visit to Heidelberg.

His ideas

Parsons's aim as a sociologist was to create a general theory which would explain individual experiences by specifying all the conceptual elements which permit social actions. He tried to do this by specifying abstract propositions which in turn would lead to narrower, more specific theories. In other words, Parsons was trying to set out a grand theoretical framework which other sociologists could then apply to particular situations, rather as the grand theories of Newton or Einstein about gravity or relativity can be applied to specific problems.

The titles of some of his main books illustrate his concerns: *The Structure of Social Action, The Social System*, and *Action Theory and the Human Condition* are three of his major works and show his interest in broad, abstract areas.

Parsons was particularly concerned to explore the problem of social order. Why does society not collapse in chaos? What forces make social existence fairly orderly and to some extent predictable? One approach to these questions is given by *structural-functionalist* ideas with which Parsons was intimately concerned.

Another approach to the problem of social order adopted by Parsons was to examine *voluntarism* and the role of the individual in society. One way to do this was to use a model of what he called *pattern-variables* to analyse a situation. For example, one variable was concerned with *Universality v. Particularism*. Sometimes we evaluate people using universal standards—Is he a good enough driver to pass the Ministry of Transport test? Sometimes we use particularist standards, as when we judge our own children. Pattern variables such as these could be used to analyse social action in a wide variety of circumstances.

His importance

Because it was concerned with methods, Parsons's work provides one way for sociologists to construct an approach to proper scientific research; in other words to make sociology a science.

Parson popularized the work of earlier sociologists such as Weber and integrated their ideas into his own thinking. Partly as a consequence of this he clarified the use of vital concepts such as *role* or *social structure* which are a central part of the sociologist's vocabulary.

His ideas spread partly because many of his students adapted his ideas and propagated them when they subsequently obtained positions of influence. For several years he was the most influential living sociologist and his ideas remain influential, though they have been challenged by a resurgence of Marxist sociology.

Further reading

Because his ideas are so difficult, it is not easy to suggest introductory reading on Parsons, but Peter Hamilton (1983). *Talcott Parsons*. London: Ellis Horwood/Tavistock Publications provides a concise outline of his ideas and some biographical detail.

Childhood socialization influences the child's personality. The kind of person we become as adults is not fixed and immutable at birth; our personality changes as we grow and this potential for change is particularly great in young children. According to Parsons, the wife usually undertakes most child care and, since there is more affinity between womenfolk, the result is often 'good girls' and 'naughty boys'. Parsons sees the family as being the only institution in society which can provide the love and care needed to allow the human personality to develop to its optimum level.

The second socializing function of the family according to Parsons concerns adults. For a time in adolescence young people may reject the family and its values. Determined to 'find themselves', they may explore new ideas and beliefs, and ways of living that are different from those of their parents. However, as they mature, most will revert to the ways of their parents. Parsons was less concerned with adolescence than with the emotional stability existing between the married partners of the family. Men may be separated from their wives by their work, whilst women in nuclear families may feel isolated from their kin because they live in different areas. As the children grow up the married couple look to each other for emotional support. This can be particularly important for men, because when they retire they often face a completely different way of life. For most women retirement will not affect their domestic role. A stable family will facilitate the emotional adjustments that are an inevitable part of human life.

Parson's views on the family exemplify a social science perspective called *functionalism*. This was originally derived from anthropologists who saw the culture of any society as a single entity where each part was linked to all the others and so helped to maintain stability in society. If any part was disrupted, then other parts of the system would be upset. Particular institutions of the social structure, such as the family, can therefore be analysed to see what contribution they make to a successful functioning of the system as a whole, rather as the parts of a living organism can be studied to see what parts they play in its existence. For example, rituals in a society — such as the coronation of a King or the opening of a parliament — are useful to a society because they help to reinforce shared values and so maintain solidarity between different groups in the society. Rituals serve their function even though those taking part in the ritual do not realize this purpose. In this way functionalism lets social scientists look beneath the obvious explanations of social life and so examine society in new ways. For example, the obvious function of a student rag may be to raise money for charity; its hidden function may be more concerned with friendship formation or breaking social conventions by behaving in mildly outrageous ways. Similarly the major rituals of family life such as weddings and funerals function at two levels. In addition to their obvious purpose they serve to bind together members of the family and, in the case of funerals, to assuage grief.

Functionalism has often been criticized as a conservative approach because it concentrates on the maintenance of social life and institutions and neglects the elements of conflict and coercion in social institutions such as the family. These critics emphasize marital breakdown such as divorce and separation and the dysfunctional effects of the family.

Marxists offer the most substantial opposition to the functionalist perspective and they stress the desirability of change in the family. For Marxists the family is particularly concerned with political socialization. The family generally turns people's interests away from outside influences such as the trade unions or class solidarity. It also tries to socialize the young into accepting the existing social and political system. If it is successful, then the members of the family are never really conscious that alternative forms of social and political organization are possible. Thus, the family usually socializes the young into accepting the status quo—though of course in some families children are socialized into political awareness.

Families differ in the way they perform their socializing function, in part because they differ in the value they place on certain qualities, and partly because they use differing techniques to secure compliance. Social class was discussed in earlier chapters in the context of work and political participation, but class also seems to influence the way in which parents bring up their children. Research in Britain and in the U S A (Newson 1970, Bronfenbrenner 1958) suggests that parents in manual occupations are more likely to use physical forms of punishment whilst parents in non-manual occupations were less likely to use corporal punishment, and instead used verbal control and spent more time explaining to children why they ought not to do certain things. These middle-class parents were less concerned with neatness and quietness and tried to ensure that their children understood the reasons why they should or should not do certain acts in order to encourage self-control. The causes of these differences between classes are not known for certain. It may be that middle-class parents have larger homes and can therefore tolerate more disorder, or that they are more likely to read books on child care. Another factor may be that the work experiences of non-manual parents encourage self-assessment and control in inter-personal relations whilst manual work stimulates more direct responses.

The socializing function of the family does seem to have changed, at least a little, over the years. Television, magazines, and child care books provide changing models for parents to follow. Moreover in the last hundred years specialized institutions have taken over some of the educational functions previously performed by the family. Play groups and nursery schools change not only the behaviour of children but also the way in which parents see their role. This concept of role is so important in social science that it is considered in a separate section later in the chapter.

The placement function

In some societies the individual's position in life is largely determined by birth. Prince Charles's position in life was determined when he was born. In Hindu caste society, the family has an important placement function and it is difficult—though not impossible—for people from lower status castes to rise in status and economic position. Although the caste system is weakening it has still a strong effect on the life of millions of Hindus. In this kind of society status is largely *ascribed*. On the other hand, in modern Western societies status is *achieved* and the education system has an important placement function because the kind of work individuals do depends, at least in part, on the kind of educational qualifications they possess. The family contributes to the placement function because there is a very strong relationship between parents' social class and the educational achievements of their children. The child of a barrister or surgeon will very probably obtain a better education and a higher status occupation than the child of an unemployed refuse collector. One reason for this is that parents give their children expectations about what kind of education and work is appropriate to them and they try to make it possible for these expectations to be fulfilled.

Economic functions

The family has always had an important economic function. For example, property may be held in common by members of the family and inheritance of assets is largely determined by family membership. If you sincerely want to be rich you should choose your parents with care!

In non-industrial societies the family has an important function as a unit of production. In some subsistence economies the father may hunt, the children look after the animals, whilst the wife and older daughters not only cook but also grow crops. The precise activities will of course vary with differing agriculture practice, but it is very common in many areas of the world for families to consume what they produce. Even in advanced industrial economies, farmers' families may be an essential unit of production. However, with industrialization the family tended to lose much of its importance as a unit of production as work was taken out of the domestic sphere and into factories.

The family retains an important economic function—that of consumption. Most of the money earned by family members is spent on the family—on providing food, clothes, and all the other requirements of family life. When economists are trying to predict consumer expenditure in the future, it is the family which is used as the unit of expenditure. Market researchers and advertisers make use of social science techniques and base their selling tactics on the assumption that the family is the basic unit of consumption in the modern economy.

Other functions

A number of other functions have been undertaken by the family, though some of these have now been taken over by other agencies, particularly the state. The family used to have a considerable educational function. Children were often taught to read and write at home. They may also have learnt their parents' occupational skills so that they could 'follow in father's footsteps'. Many of the educational functions have increasingly been taken over by the schools.

Similarly, the family used to be largely responsible for the health of its members. It still retains some concern for providing primary health care, but as this has become more specialized, this function has been taken over by medical personnel.

In these ways, therefore, it seems that the family may be changing its functions. In particular its activities seem to be narrowing so that it concentrates on child-bearing and socialization.

Family Roles and Relationships

When discussing the socializing function of the family reference was made to the influences which the family had on creating and reinforcing roles. Because it is such a powerful institution the family has a great influence on how we perceive the world and how we expect others to behave. In particular, we tend to expect all mothers and fathers to behave in the same way as our own mothers and fathers. There is a tendency for people to assume that the pattern of life which we see as young children is a natural one.

Concept Box 4.2 Role

In social science the word 'role' describes a bundle of expectations and obligations to act in particular ways in certain settings. These are distinct from the personal characteristics of the individual; for example, priests, waiters, or bus-drivers have to perform a professional role which may be quite different from their personal inclinations at any particular time. The expectations which accompany the role are learned as part of the socialization process so that even young children develop expectations of how mothers and fathers ought to behave. Because role play is action in conformity with a set of rules, once these rules are learned behaviour can become almost automatic and the appropriate behaviour is reinforced by the continuing pressure of other people's expectations. Sometimes these pressures are irresistible; the priest saying Mass would find it impossible to take out a pack of cards and invite the congregation to play poker. Sometimes expectations permit a good deal of latitude so that one father may behave in quite different ways to another, although if a father behaves in obviously inappropriate ways, he will receive social disapproval. If he behaves as good fathers ought to do then he will receive approval. In this way expectations shape and reinforce appropriate behaviour.

Childhood expectations are often successfully reinforced by the media so that we may unconsciously come to believe that it is natural for the father to go out to work and for the mother to stay at home and look after the children; that it is natural for girls to play with dolls and boys with motors; that women are meant to cook and men to do household repairs; that women should be concerned about the whiteness of the wash and men about the strength of the beer. This is because women are often seen by the media as naturally passive, caring, domesticated, motherly, and emotional, whilst men are presented as tough, logical, and ambitious. The key biological role of women is childbearing and her social nature is said to be derived from this so the female is designed to be loving. These 'natural' biological differences give rise to social roles:

> Man for the field and woman for the hearth;
> Man for the sword and for the needle she;
> Man with the head and woman with the heart;
> Man to command and woman to obey;
> All else confusion.
>
> (Alfred Lord Tennyson)

Social scientists other than those with an individualistic perspective are sceptical about beliefs which suggest that gender differences are 'only natural', for many of the attitudes and beliefs which we take for granted as natural are, in fact, learned and are caused by social forces. Anthropologists have played a major part in this discovery. The leading figure in this work—so far as it relates to differences between the sexes—has been Margaret Mead.

Profile 4.2 Margaret Mead (1901–1978)

Her life

Margaret Mead was born in Philadelphia on 16 December 1901. Her mother was a slightly built, determined, rather serious woman, and an ardent supporter of good causes. Her father was a professor at the University of Pennsylvania in the School of Finance. Despite this, the family was often short of money and her father was reluctant to provide money for her education.

Her schooling was erratic. 'Some years we went to school. Other years we stayed at home and Grandma taught us' she wrote in her autobiography. One reason for this was that the family lived in a different house almost every year. School provided no challenge, but 'I wanted to live out every experience that went with schooling, and so I made a best friend out of the most likely candidate, fell sentimentally in love with one of the boys, attached myself to a teacher, and organised as far as it was possible to do so, every kind of game, play, performance . . .'

At college she had an active social and intellectual life with a group of girls calling themselves the 'Ash Can Cats'. She studied a number of subjects, mainly psychology, before turning to anthropology. Whilst still a student she married her first husband, Luther Cressman, though she decided to keep her own name. The marriage lasted only four years.

Her first field trip was to Samoa when she was 24 and this was followed by other trips to the South Seas, particularly New Guinea which at that time was still very primitive, only recently refraining from head hunting. These trips involved living in quite rough circumstances. Returning from one trip she met her second husband who was also an anthropologist. This marriage also did not last, and in 1935 she married her third husband, Gregory Bateson, who was also an anthropologist. They had one child, a daughter, who was the source of much joy and who eventually made her a doting grandmother.

During the Second World War Mead was a member of a team which made studies of national cultures for the US government. For most of her life she was on the staff of the American Museum of National History and taught at Columbia and other universities. She revisited New Guinea and other South Sea islands and wrote a large number of books and articles—over 1,400 in total. She died in November 1978.

Her ideas

Mead wrote 'I went to Samoa—as, later, I went to other societies on which I have worked—to find out more about human beings, human beings like ourselves in everything except their culture. Through accidents of history, these cultures had developed so differently from ours that knowledge of these could shed a kind of light on us, upon our potentialities and our limitations, that was unique.' In all her work, she sought to relate patterns of living in other cultures to the current practice in America. Thus on her first field trip she sought to discover whether adolescence was an experience specific to American and similar cultures or whether it was a universal manifestation resulting from biological changes which resulted in disruptive behaviour. The picture she presented of relaxed, sexually free, Samoan girls suggested that the problems of adolescence were caused by culture not biology.

Mead also studied the natures of 'male' and 'female' with similar results. Her work suggested that what we call 'human nature' is not fixed and that cultural conditions and environmental forces can be more important than biology in deciding what kind of people are found in a society. Since cultural factors can be changed by people, it follows that 'human nature' can be changed.

Her importance

Although Mead's work has been criticized by some anthropologists, her conclusions have been generally accepted.

Apart from the mass of data she provided on 'her' Pacific peoples—for example, Mead and her husband Bateson took 25,000 photographs on one fieldwork trip in Bali—her interpretations of her observations have changed the way in which people think about human nature. This influence was not limited to social scientists for she was a superb popularizer of anthropology and became the most famous anthropologist in the world.

Further reading

Her autobiography Blackberry Winter. (1973). London: Angus and Robertson gives a very readable picture of her life until the Second World War. All her books are well written and interesting to the non-specialist. Coming of Age in Samoa. (1971), Male and Female. (1970), and Growing up in New Guinea. (1970), (all Penguin) are easily available. These works are criticized in Derek Freeman's book Margaret Mead and Samoa. (1984). Harmondsworth: Penguin.

Mead studied a number of societies in the South Pacific and claimed that behaviour which was regarded as natural in one society would be considered as unnatural in another, so that there is no universal role which is masculine or feminine. Anthropologists have found that in some societies it is the women who take on the characteristics we associate with men, such as domination and aggression, while men are complaint, gentle, and caring. Similarly, the women in some societies do all the agricultural work because it is assumed that they are stronger than the men. Margaret Mead's work suggested that in Arapesh (in New Guinea) both men and women were expected to be succouring and cherishing and equally concerned with the growth of children. Aggressive behaviour by either sex was heavily discouraged. Another tribe, the Mundugumor, were a great contrast. Both men and women were expected to be positively sexed and aggressive. As in Arapesh both men and women were expected to conform to a single type; the idea of different behaviour patterns for men and women was completely alien. Among the Tchambuli the expected relations between men and women reversed those often expected in the West. The women were brisk and hearty, managed the business affairs of life, and took control of the valuables. The men painted and gossiped, were catty, jealous, had temper tantrums, and the women chose which men they fancied as sexual partners.

Thus it is clear that characteristics which we may consider to be natural are, in fact, learned. In other words, social pressures affect boys and girls so that they take on appropriate behaviours. The message of anthropology is clear: a large part of our social behaviour is defined by the society in which we live; different social roles would be appropriate in other societies. One generalization which can be made is that in most societies the activities which are generally undertaken by men tend to be regarded as being more important or having higher status than those undertaken by women. For example, if a woman is asked what she does she may reply 'I'm only a housewife.'

Method Box 4.3 Participant Observation

Participant observation is a method of research used particularly by anthropologists, sociologists, and social psychologists. It contrasts with other methods such as the use of laboratory experiments, questionnaires, or interviews. Observation gives rise to a wide variety of data, including some which may be completely unexpected when the observation begins. Participant observers place themselves in the life of the community so that they can observe over a period of time what people do. The community studied may vary widely from South Sea islanders to Chicago street gangs, medical students, or prisoners. It is a lengthy process; the observer may have to learn a new language and will certainly have to spend long periods in becoming accepted as a member of the group to be studied. The observer then records interactions in order to answer questions such as Who talks to whom? How are leaders chosen? How are decisions made? Who carries them out? What kind of people have high/low status? How do ideas spread? How are sanctions applied to those who break the rules? From observations such as these models can be built and theories developed. Apart from the long period involved in undertaking such studies there are a number of other problems. It is difficult to observe some areas of society—such as the family—because it is hard to become accepted as a member of the group. Secondly, there may be a problem of bias. Observers often see what they expect to see and so may come away with their preconceptions reinforced. More subtly, they may come to like the group they are observing and so seek to give a good picture by ignoring or playing down those aspects which could cause the group to be criticized. Moreover the very presence of an observer may modify the behaviour being observed. There are also ethical problems. For example, the observer may misrepresent his or her true purpose to gain acceptability by the group, or may incite the group to do something interesting for the observer which they would regret.

Despite these difficulties, participant observation has a long and distinguished history as a technique of social research undertaken by anthropologists such as Margaret Mead and also by sociologists. It has been proved to be of greatest use in the study of topics for which survey evidence is unobtainable or unreliable and where very little is known about a subject.

Husband and wife play out roles and marriage is a situation where inequality persists. We talk about 'man and wife', never 'woman and husband'. The very phrase 'man and wife' indicates inequality, for the wife is seen as the appendage of the man. Marriage defines a woman's place whereas it has little effect on a man's status.

Despite great differences between families it is possible to generalize about gender roles within the family. The classic traditional pattern in working-class communities such as miners or dockers was that men were the bread-winners and spent much of their leisure time in social organizations catering largely for men, such as pubs or at sporting events like football matches or horse-racing. Other hobbies, such as pigeon-racing, were also for men only. At home, the men undertook little or no domestic work and considered child care to be women's work. This account is of course something of a caricature but it represents a life-style which still affects patterns of living, despite social changes which may have modified the life-styles of working men. The spread of home ownership, longer holidays, shorter working weeks, and, more recently, large scale unemployment, have encouraged men to spend more time at home where they are more likely to undertake household chores than their fathers used to do. This is particularly probable if the wife goes out to work. These changes may be seen as threatening by some men because they undermine male dominance of the home and require new skills and attitudes to be learned. Moreover a working wife may try to require her husband to undertake chores which he would rather not perform. Change in roles frequently induces tension and changes in such central roles as husband and wife can cause considerable upsets.

On the surface at least the role of women has changed considerably in the last few decades. Traditionally, 'woman's place is in the home'. That is, a woman's primary role has been seen to be concerned with caring for children and husband and with carrying out domestic chores such as cooking and cleaning. To many people this role is seen as deriving naturally from women's physical make-up because only the female can bear children or breast-feed them. Deviations from this role may be threatening or comic. Situation comedies on television exploit role reversal where the man wears the pinafore and the woman is bossy. In this way, comedy may relieve situations which people find threatening.

The view that women's role should be confined to domestic chores is, in fact, relatively recent; it is largely a product of industrialization. In pre-industrial societies the roles of men and women were more similar than they are today. Women expected to continue productive work when they married and whether this work was in agriculture, textiles, or in trade made little difference. Consequently, the woman was less dependent on her husband's earnings. Women did not have to choose between productive work and domesticity. It was largely the development of an industrial society which restricted women to the home so that the home became separated from the economy. The duties undertaken by women in the home came to be seen as second-rate work. Marxist sociologists in particular have developed this argument to suggest that the material base for subordination of women lies in their exclusion from economic production. This economic subordination affects socialization patterns so that in the family girls learn character traits such as passivity and subordination which reinforce the economic dependence.

In these circumstances the extended family took on another role in many societies as a kind of women's trade union. This could occur even in the large cities of industrialized societies because a married couple often started their married life in close proximity to the wife's mother. This meant that the newly married woman could call on her mother for help in running a house when there was illness or childbirth. It also helped to reduce the isolation felt by many women cut off from the world of work.

The Women's Movement—sometimes called feminism—originated largely in the U S A in the 1960s but spread rapidly to other countries. Although there are a number of differing opinions and groups within the feminist movement the essential foundation of their beliefs is that women are unequal not because of differences in physical or mental capacities but because forces in society make them unequal. They seek to overcome this subordination in a number of ways. One strand of the movement seeks to cut itself off from male society and so encourages female communal life outside the family. More usually women's groups press for equal opportunities for women to obtain work and to be promoted at work. This implies men taking on a fair share of domestic duties.

It is not possible to decide to what extent this movement has been successful. There certainly seems to be evidence—discussed later—that woman's role is changing but whether this change is caused by protest groups or by other changes in society is not easy to determine. This difficulty should not surprise social scientists. Human society is so complex that almost any change is difficult to analyse in terms of cause and effect. If a Republican President is elected in the U S A is this because he is a skilled campaigner or because of the incompetence of his opponents; because the media tend to support Republicans or because changes in the economy have made Republican policies popular? If there is a decline in tribalism in Nigeria is that because economic forces help unify the country, because tribalism is seen as outdated, because political leaders have sought to restrict its importance, or for some other reason? Social science can rarely give clear and simple answers to questions such as those concerned with changes in society, partly because these changes often interact and reinforce each other. In the case of the Women's Movement it may simply be that it helped intensify changes that were already underway in society.

Role of the child

Much has been written about the changing role of women, but the child's role is also changing. Children not only cause changes in the pattern of family life, but the way in which children are treated in the family will have a deep effect on their future lives.

The way in which adults perceive children has changed over time. Before the industrial revolution a woman might expect to bear over a dozen children, many of whom would die either at birth or whilst still very young. Married couples wanted lots of children in the hope that some would survive and whilst the death of a child was sad, it was not unexpected.

Childhood in this society was brief and children given relatively little attention. There were few toys, little children's literature, and children usually wore small versions of adult clothes. They were seen as small adults and treated as such. They were quickly expected to help look after the younger members of the family, to help in the fields, and in the home. As young as seven or eight they may have left home to work as servants in other houses, as apprentices, or for their parents. Infancy was but a brief interlude before the adult world began.

When the domestic system was replaced by industrialization, children's role changed. At first they were sent out to work long hours in the new factories. Their labour was cheap and they were often more flexible in attitude than older people who were more accustomed to field than factory. Gradually attitudes towards child labour changed. Laws were passed which restricted the number of hours a child could work. Around 1870 in many European countries laws were passed which made education compulsory. The spread of clean water, public sewers, and better medical knowledge reduced child mortality. These changes caused children's lives to be different. They became bread eaters without being bread-winners (Young and Willmott 1973, p. 74). As children's work became less important their play became more important. Children were no longer viewed as little adults but as individuals in their own right, with childhood recognized as a separate and important stage in development. Children's toys were produced in great quantity. Christmas developed as a children's festival. Parents—usually mothers—began to give far more care to the upbringing of their children and large numbers of books were published on child care.

It was recognized that the way children were treated in the family would have a profound effect on their future personalities. Children are socialized in a variety of ways not fully understood, but one of these is that they identify with their parents and try to behave in similar ways. A girl may see her mother cooking and cleaning, a boy watch his father going out to work or mending the car, and they come to believe that these are the proper roles for women and men respectively. These values are *internalized* by the child so that these gender roles are seen as natural. Of course gender roles in most families are more complex than this, and subsequent experience may modify childhood learning, but it is in childhood that we learn from our parents the appropriate behaviours and activities suitable for men and for women.

This is one way in which we are socialized into accepting stereotypes so that we come to believe that certain types of behaviour are appropriate to each sex. When we see people behaving in ways which conform to our stereotype we are reassured and the stereotype is reinforced.

One consequence of the 'invention' of childhood as a separate stage was that the shift from childhood to adulthood became uncertain and troubled. In some parts of the world young people undergo ceremonies—rites of passage—which may take several weeks, in which they learn adult behaviour, perform rituals, and at the end emerge as adults, treated as such by other adults. In most western countries the passage from child to adult is less easy. Adolescence is often a time of trauma; young people wishing to be treated as adults yet behaving with childhood uncertainties. It is always difficult to change roles, and the change from child to adult, from boy to man, and from girl to woman is fraught with difficulty.

Is the family changing?

It is clear that changes have taken place in the roles of men, women, and children. What is less certain is the *extent* of these changes. Have they substantially changed the role and function of the family, or have these changes been relatively trivial? Is the family still one of the most important social institutions or is it declining in influence? And if it is declining, what effect will this have on society?

In Victorian times the family was seen as central to society. At its head was the father: stern, perhaps a little remote, responsible for providing for the family, and perhaps rather distant from the children who were the responsibility of the mother. As there were many children and little domestic machinery to make work easy, this was a considerable burden. The mother was responsible for the social training of the child, though the father would become involved in important matters such as choice of jobs for the children. Children were to be seen and not heard. They were supposed to be polite and respectful to their elders. Widowed grandparents may have lived with, or near, the family, helping to care for the young ones and in turn being cared for as they grew too old to look after themselves. The family was to be self-reliant, standing on its own feet without help from the state. People were responsible for the consequences of their actions.

So much for the stereotype. Like all stereotypes it contains an element of truth, but is a distortion of reality. Few families conformed to this pattern. Nevertheless the stereotype is useful because it helps us to consider not only the changes which have occured in the family but also the changes which people *think* have happened.

Family stability

If the Victorian family had one quality above all the others, it was thought to be stability. There was little divorce; marriage was 'till death us do part' so that children were reared in a stable environment which ensured that they learnt and practised proper values. The evils of the present day are seen by some as arising because families now split up. Divorce and illegitimacy are prevalent so that children lack stable life and so are liable to become delinquent, rejecting society's values.

It is certainly true that there has been an increase in the number of divorces. In the two decades following 1961 the number of divorces in the U K rose from 27,000 to 157,000 so that by the early 1980s about 170,000 children under 16 were affected each year by their parents divorcing (Social Trends 1984 Tables 2. 14, 2. 16). The position in the U K is not exceptional as Table 4.2 shows.

Divorce rates vary between countries for a variety of reasons. In particular, the law concerning divorce varies between countries. In some divorce is easily available and cheap; in others almost impossible. The law also changes over time. For example, before 1857 divorce in Britain required a separate Act of Parliament for each divorce—a procedure that was extremely expensive and difficult. Even after 1857 it was impossible for all except the fairly rich to obtain a divorce. Religious beliefs also affect the incidence of

Table 4.2. Divorce Rates (1983)[1]

Country	Rate[2]
Bermuda	5.5
Canada	2.9
USA	5.0
Japan	1.4
France	1.6
FRG	1.9
Italy	0.2
UK	2.8
Australia	2.8
New Zealand	3.0
USSR	3.5

[1] For some countries the data refer to earlier years.
[2] Rates are the number of final divorce decrees granted under civil law per 1000 of the population.

Source: United Nations Demographic Yearbook New York (1983).

divorce, either by influencing the severity or otherwise of the law or by affecting the altitudes of people towards divorce whatever the law. Divorce rates are usually low in Catholic countries for this reason.

There are a number of causes for this increase in divorce. In many countries it has become easier and cheaper. There is now little or no stigma attached to those who are divorced and religious opposition is less pronounced. Because women are more likely to possess educational qualifications and to go to work, they feel more able to take care of themselves and so less likely to tolerate an unhappy marriage. Moreover the trend to smaller families means that there are fewer children to take into consideration.

An increase in the number of divorces has led to an increase in the number of one-parent families. Since divorce courts usually give custody to the mother, the typical one-parent family consists of mother and children rather than father and children.

These changes cause concern to those who stress the importance of the family in maintaining social stability. If families break up today, might not society do so tomorrow? It is sometimes argued that parents whose children are divorced may be less well socialized and in turn may find it difficult in later life to maintain their own marriages. This may be because children learn the role of husband/

father and wife/mother from their parents. If one parent is absent these roles will be difficult to perform in later life.

Reality is more complex than this over-simplified picture suggests. The Victorian family was not a model of stability. In the British census of 1857 18 per cent of all households containing children and a household head who was aged less than 65 were single-parent households. This was double the rate of a century later (Anderson 1983). The main reason for the large number of one-parent families in Victorian times was not divorce but death. Of the couples who married in the 1860s about one in three had their marriage broken by death within twenty years. Children were more likely to come from a broken home in the 1870s than in the 1970s. Moreover many of the marriages which survived must have been unhappy. Although some couples separated, because divorce was extremely difficult unhappy couples usually stayed together so that many children were brought up in homes with marital problems. If the ideal family is one where children are brought up by two caring parents in a loving, happy atmosphere, this is more likely to occur today than a century ago.

Another reason for the existence of one-parent families is illegitimacy. In the last twenty years in Britain the proportion of illegitimate births has more than doubled so that 19 per cent of all live births are to unmarried women (Social Trends 1986). Again this is used as evidence for the decline of the family.

The statistics can be misleading. In some cases the parents of the illegitimate child are living together as husband and wife, even though unmarried. In others they will subsequently marry or the mother will marry a man who will care for the child as his own. Some illegitimate children will be adopted. In all these cases the child will be brought up in a 'family' with a mother and father. Even in Victorian times when sexual morality was given such great emphasis, many children were born out of wedlock so that the difference between then and now can easily be exaggerated. The family seems to be a remarkably stable institution.

Number of children

The character of a family is heavily influenced by the number of children in it. Although there are variations between countries it is clear that there has been a fall in family size in the industrial countries. A century ago the average number of children born into each family in these countries was about 6; by 1900 it had fallen to 3.3,

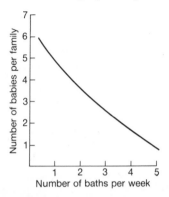

Fig. 4.1 Babies and Baths

and in several countries today there are less than 2 children in the average family.

In the developing world the situation is very different and family size is large, though here again there are great differences between countries. In China, for example, the government tries to restrict each married couple to one child in order to restrict population growth. (When the number of children per married couple falls below two the population will eventually fall if there is no net immigration. Indeed since some people do not marry, the average number of children per married couple needs to exceed two in order to maintain a stable level of population.)

Explaining the trend to smaller families can be used to illustrate how difficult it is to prove cause and effect in social life. As the (hypothetical) data in Figure 4.1 show, a century ago people had few baths and many children. Now the position is reversed, and families have many baths and few children. Does this mean that bathing is a successful contraceptive? Or that people have fewer children because they spend so long in the bath that they have no time for sex? Alas, the truth is more prosaic. Although the two trends show a statistical link called correlation, this does not prove cause and effect. People have more baths because rising living standards mean that more people have bathrooms and hot running water. So far as the fall in the number of children is concerned, there are a number of interlocking reasons:

- Better contraceptives, more easily available together with less religious opposition to contraception.

- As school leaving ages have risen, the costs of bringing up children have risen because children at school cannot earn.

- The state takes a greater role in caring for old people; more old people will receive pensions, so children are not needed as insurance for old age.

- People want fewer children because rising medical standards mean that those that are born are expected to live to maturity.

- Women's expectations have changed; in particular they expect to return to work after bringing up children and this is difficult to do with many children.

Changes in the number of children in a family have a considerable effect on the life-style of the members. In small families, people tend to have more space. More importantly, each child will have relatively more contact with the adult members of the family since the parents will have fewer calls on the limited time available. This should ensure more effective socialization of the child and perhaps also help children to do well at school. Children in small families may also be better off financially.

Working wives

The stereotype of a wife is a woman caring for a home and family, with few concerns outside this limited area. A generation ago the stereotype may have contained some truth—for example, in some occupations women were compelled to give up their work when they married. Even then, in some industries such as cotton it was common for married women to go out to work. Nowadays the typical pattern is for a woman to continue in paid employment after marriage until a few weeks before the birth of her first child. She may then have a second child a couple of years later and seek to return to paid employment when these reach school age, though at first the work may be part time. In some cases grandparents or an au pair or child-minder will make it possible for the mother to return to employment earlier. In others the mother may prefer to stay at home or may be unable to obtain work. In Britain about half the mothers with children age 5–9 years go out to work either full or part time and the figure is much higher for mothers of older children

(Nissell 1982). These figures are replicated in most other industrial countries.

The trend towards more mothers working has been made possible in part by the fall in family size. A woman with many children finds it much more difficult to undertake paid employment than one with few children. This does not fully explain the trend to paid employment. Women are seeking greater fulfilment than can be obtained by being 'only a housewife'. As the chapter on work explained, people seek employment for more than money; they seek satisfaction, for example that provided by social interaction.

Nevertheless money remains a prime motive for women to go out to work. Though they are sometimes accused of working for 'pin-money', married women's earnings contribute substantially to the family standard of living. A family with one income may be poor; a family with two incomes will be able to afford some luxuries. Domestic appliances such as the washing machine save time and make it possible to go out to work and thus to buy such items.

Taking a broader perspective, a large part of the economic growth experienced by most countries since the Second World War has been due to the extra output produced by working wives. The economy needs the contribution made by married women, without it the National Income of every country would collapse.

Women workers tend to be concentrated in certain occupations, often concerned with 'caring' roles such as nursing, or related to domestic activity such as cleaning or teaching young children, or serving men, for example as secretaries. In every country women on average earn less than men, and this is the case even within the same occupation. Women's unequal position in employment is partly a consequence of their position in the family. If their primary concern is for the home then their contribution to work may be seen to justify lower status and pay. Women form a cheap, relatively unorganized source of labour which has led Marxists to suggest that in capitalist societies women form a 'reserve army of labour'. They can be used as cheap labour at times of war or when the economy is booming and can be easily discarded at other times.

Whatever the reasons for women seeking paid employment the effects on the family are considerable. The role of 'wife' changes. Instead of being solely concerned with domestic affairs the wife becomes a 'worker' as well. She plays two roles and this can cause *role conflict*. This is the phrase used by sociologists when a person plays parts in which people's expectations for each role are not in agreement. For example, a policeman is expected to uphold the law and as an individual is expected to help family and friends. If he finds a close relative breaking the law these expectations will conflict and be difficult to resolve. In the case of working mothers there is often considerable role conflict. As a mother she is expected to care for her home and family. As an employee she is expected to perform her work to the same standard as men or unmarried women. Conflicts can easily arise—if her child is ill, if her employers expect her to work overtime, or if her work makes her tired so that she cannot perform her household duties as she would wish.

These conflicts can be resolved in several ways. She may 'resolve' them by working twice as hard, by omitting some household duties or by restricting her contribution at work. Alternatively other members of her family may take up some of the domestic duties.

A good deal of attention has focused on the effects on the children of working mothers. Do the children suffer if their mother goes out to work? Research in this area has been undertaken by a number of people (Willmott and Willmott 1982) who have typically studied a number of children whose mothers are in paid employment and compared them to otherwise similar children (e.g. similar in age, sex, social class, and family size and income) whose mothers do not go out to work. The research suggests that whether the mother works or not in the pre-school years does not affect the child's emotional or social adjustment. The precise effects will vary with the circumstances and in particular with the quality and continuity of the alternative care provided. If this is good, children receiving substitute care are often more outgoing and self-confident. Similarly, children of school age whose mother goes out to work do not seem to suffer, particularly if the mother does not feel guilty about working and if adequate household arrangements can be made.

These arrangements often involve changes to the role of the father, because changes in the role of the wife involves changes in expectations about the activities of the husband. These changes seem to involve the husband taking on some of the duties that would otherwise be undertaken by the wife.

Young and Willmott (1973) have attempted to classify various stages in the development of the family. Stage 1 was pre-industrial. The family was usually the unit of production and, for the most part, men, women, and children worked together in home and field. This stage lasted until it was overtaken by industralization. In stage 2 specialization disturbed the usual relation between husband and wife so that work and family became separated. The men worked, the women stayed at home.

Stage 3 started early in the twentieth century and is still in progress. It has three main characteristics. Parents spend more time at home, especially when the children are young. Life has become more 'privatized'. Secondly, the nuclear family counts for more, the extended family for less. Thirdly, inside the marriage the roles of the sexes have become less segregated leading to a *symmetrical family*. The essence of a symmetrical relationship is that it is opposite, but similar. Technology has made the home a more pleasant place to be in. Feminism has led to greater equality. These changes have caused the family to become more domestic, with husband and wife playing roles that are increasingly similar, though clearly not identical.

Conclusion

Social scientists have focused a lot of attention on the family because it is such a powerful institution which affects the lives of individuals both as children and as adults. If the family is changing, then its influence on people will change; in particular if the family is declining then the fear is expressed that the functions carried out by the family will not be adequately performed and so society will bear the consequences.

The analysis in this chapter seems to suggest that the family is indeed changing because society itself is changing. If the changes of the last few decades continue, the symmmetry of the family will become complete. Instead of two jobs for the wife (one at work and one at home) and one for the husband, both will have two jobs. There will be continuing strains on the family, and perhaps more divorces. This may weaken the family but increasing domesticity and use of home technology may allow more time to be spent with each child so that the family performs a narrower range of functions, but with greater effect.

References

Anderson, M. (1983). 'How Much has the Family Changed?' *New Society* 27 Oct. pp. 143–6.

Bronfenbrenner, E. (1959). 'Socialization and Social Class'. In E. Maccoby, T. Newcomb, and E. Hartley (eds.). *Readings in Social Psychology*. London: Methuen.

Burgess, E. W., and H. J. Locke (1953). *The Family*. New York: Van Nostrand & Reinhold.

Hamilton P. (1983). *Talcott Parsons*. London: Ellis Horwood/Tavistock Publications.

HMSO. (1984 and 1985). *Social Trends*. London.

Leach, E. R. (1968). *A Runaway World*. London: BBC.

Murdock, G. P. (1949). *Social Structure*. London: Macmillan.

Newson, J. and E. (1970). *Four Years Old in an Urban Community*. Harmondsworth: Penguin.

Nissell, M. (1982). 'Families and Social Change Since the Second World War'. In R. N. Rapoport, M. P. Fogarty, and R. Rapoport (eds.). *Families in Britain*. London: Routledge and Kegan Paul.

Nobbs, J. (1983). *Sociology in Context*. London: Macmillan.

United Nations. (1983). *Demographic Yearbook*. New York.

Willmott, P. and P. (1982). 'Children and Family Diversity'. In Rapoport *et al.* (1982). (See Nissell (1982)).

Young, M. and P. Willmott (1973). *Symmetrical Family*. London: Routledge and Kegan Paul.

Further reading

Diana Gibbons (1985). *The Family in Question*. London: Macmillan is a readable introduction to this topic, whilst Rapoport *et al.* (1982) (See above, Nissell (1982)) is a collection of twenty-six articles about various aspects of the family.

5 Friendship, Liking, and Love

Social psychology investigates a vast array of human social activities, thoughts and feelings, ranging from the circumstances under which people will or will not help a stranger in distress, through the effects of different kinds of building design on well-being, to processes of conflict and bargaining between social groups. This chapter looks at how social psychologists study friendship, firstly because the topic exemplifies very well the central interest of social psychology in the ways that individuals react to each other and interact in social settings; secondly, because there is a great deal of work going on in the area at present; and finally, because friends and friendship matter to almost everyone.

For the purposes of this chapter friendship is considered to be a long-term, voluntary, affectionate relationship between two individuals. This includes heterosexual and homosexual love relationships, as well as the perhaps less exciting but often more long-lasting friendships between school companions, workmates, and neighbours. Differences undoubtedly exist between the former 'loving' relationships and the latter group based more, perhaps, on 'liking', but there are also many similarities, enough to justify our lumping them all within the category of 'friendships' or 'personal relationships' to use the term that most researchers prefer.

Through history and across cultures friendships have varied, and still vary very much in their typical activities, and in the importance of friendships in people's lives relative to other commitments, such as the family; however, voluntary bonds outside the kinship network are found in all cultures and at all historical periods, and are a central aspect of most societies. Children can identify their 'friends' and those with whom they are 'not friends' from as early as three to four years of age; although the functions and forms of children's friendships seem to change rapidly during childhood there is no doubt that the child's relationships with other children outside the family increase in importance as he or she grows older. By early adolescence friendships are usually the most significant component of the individual's social life: studies in North America, Western Europe, the USSR, and Japan all find a marked reduction in the importance of kinship ties in favour of friendship bonds in adolescence, although this feature is not so evident in less economically developed, more traditional cultures. Friendships and intimate sexual relationships remain pivotal features of social life throughout adulthood, although most research activity has concentrated on the marital relationship, to the relative exclusion of other types. This is unfortunate but perhaps understandable, given the high visibility and social significance of marriage in most societies, and the amount of public concern that exists about issues of marital breakdown, divorce, and their effects on children. Marriage, however, does not normally exist in a social vacuum, and some recent research has begun to look at the interplay between a marriage and the other kinship and friendship ties that the spouses maintain; it is suggested that the progress or decline of a marriage can be fully understood only when the constructive or destructive contributions from the couple's whole network of other relationships are taken into account.

Another welcome development in recent research has been an increasing interest in the role of friendship in middle and old age. Indications are that friendship may take on a new importance as family ties weaken with the departure of grown-up children, or are broken by death of spouse or by divorce. Loneliness due to loss or lack of friends is a commonly reported feature of old age, although it is by no means restricted to that age group.

Friendship For What?

Friendships help us to satisfy many of our most basic social needs. They provide a feeling of belonging and a sense of social identity; the old saying 'show me your friends and I'll tell you what you are' reflects one aspect of friendship which emerges very clearly in the replies of adolescents to research questions. Furthermore to be the friend of an admired and popular person confers status and importance upon the individual amongst those who matter most, the peer group. To have a friend is also to be liked, approved of, and esteemed, and to have one's outlook on things supported and confirmed: thus one's self-esteem is enhanced and bolstered.

Concept Box 5.1 Self-concept and Self-esteem

The idea of 'the self' is an extremely complex notion both in philosophy and in psychology, but most psychologists use the term 'self-concept' to refer to the image a person holds of him or herself. This includes such things as body image (how I see myself physically) as well as my assessment of my intellectual and practical abilities, my popularity or otherwise, and my view of my own attitudes, values, traits, temperament, and ambitions; in short, just about every item that goes to make up my picture of myself, in my mind's eye. This self-concept changes with age and experience, and may become very complex; so some elaborate methods have been developed to measure the self-concept, since the ability to measure is a prerequisite for a scientific understanding of anything.

The aspect of the self-concept that has been of most interest to social psychologists is self-esteem, the extent to which I like or dislike, approve or disapprove, of myself. This also may be quite complex; it is quite possible for an individual to approve of one aspect of him or herself and heartily dislike another aspect. Many psychologists, however, support the notion of a *global* level of self-esteem, an overall evaluation of oneself as positive or negative—which may have both long-term and short-term characteristics. In other words, I may typically think quite well of myself, but a set-back or a social rejection may temporarily induce a negative self-evaluation. A variety of questionnaires and other devices have been developed to measure global self-esteem, and there is evidence that level of self-esteem can exert powerful effects on many aspects of our behaviour, such as willingness to take risks, attentiveness to others, and need for social approval.

Our intimate relationships, both in childhood and as adults, are seen by many researchers as being fundamental to the development and maintenance of adequate levels of self-esteem.

Friends also provide help, practical advice and support, and valuable social contacts. In addition, through our friends we learn a wide range of social knowledge: what is expected, and what is appropriate and inappropriate behaviour in particular situations; through our friendship activities we learn how we stand in terms of abilities, achievements, and know-how. There is a degree of consensus amongst friendship researchers that in the broadest sense our personal relationships enable us to maintain a sense of self-worth and develop the confidence and skills necessary to function in the social environment.

The importance of friendship is underlined by the findings of recent investigations into the effects of the breakdown and dissolution of friendships upon the individuals concerned; both physical and psychological ill-effects have been identified. In a major review of this area, Bloom, Asher, and White in 1978 found that over a wide range of psychiatric and physical illnesses separated and divorced people were very much more at risk than married or single individuals. Persons who had experienced recent marital breakdown were more likely than the rest of the population to have problems with alcoholism, to be involved in motor vehicle accidents, or to commit suicide; separated and divorced persons' risk of death by homicide was up to *seven times* greater than the risk for the population as a whole! These kinds of data are correlational, of course, so they cannot *prove* that relationship breakdown causes all these misfortunes; it is probably the case, for example, that certain kinds of personalities predisposed to psychiatric disturbance are also unable to maintain successful marriages. Overall, however, the evidence is fairly compelling: loss of a very significant personal relationship, such as marriage, produces a great deal of stress in the individual. It is interesting to note, incidentally, that in terms of the evidence collected by Bloom and his colleagues, and by others, men consistently suffer significantly greater ill-effects from the breakdown of marriage than do women.

The Scientific Study of Friendship

A few social psychologists displayed an interest in personal relationships, particularly marriage, as long ago as the 1930s, but it was in the late 1950s that systematic, theoretically-based work in the area commenced. Even then, however, only a minority of researchers actually looked at *real* long-term relationships; most preferred to work on the factors involved in people's attraction to strangers. At that time social psychology was almost totally dominated by one method of research, the laboratory experiment, and it was probably inevitable that attention would be focused on an aspect of personal relationships which could be adapted to the laboratory setting.

Method Box 5.1 Social Psychology Experiments

Although people use the word 'experiment' very loosely to describe almost any kind of scientific enquiry, in fact the experiment is a very specific type of investigation. What sets the experiment apart is that the experimenter actually manipulates and interferes with naturally occurring events in some systematic way, and observes the results. To that extent the experiment goes beyond merely observing natural events: it makes events happen, so that they can be observed. From the very beginnings of scientific psychology in the late nineteenth century psychologists have adopted the laboratory experiment as their premier research method, and so it has remained. Social psychology, as a branch of the parent discipline, followed this lead—in the 1960s over 80 per cent of articles in the most prestigious social psychological research journals were reports of experimental studies. A certain amount of scientific snobbishness contributed to the dominance of experiments in social psychology—if the most sophisticated sciences, physics and chemistry, could achieve their greatest advances through experimentation, then psychology might follow suit.

Critics of the extensive use of experiments in social psychology have pointed out that the kinds of things social psychologists study are much more vaguely defined, more complex, and uncontrollable than in the physical and biological sciences, and that to attempt to bring social phenomena into the laboratory is to risk over-simplifying them to the point of distortion.

Experiments, however, remain a very popular method of research in social psychology. Advocates of the approach point to some major advantages in their use. Firstly, experiments enable us to identify which is the *cause* and which the *effect* in a social process; this is usually very difficult to do when one merely observes natural events in all their bewildering complexity, or when one interviews people about past events. By systematically manipulating some factor, controlling the potential effects of other factors, and observing subsequent events, the experimenter hopes to establish clearly which causes what in social phenomena. Secondly, experiments, being relatively simple and artificial, are capable of being repeated by other investigators in other laboratories, in a way that real life events never can: no riot, for instance, is quite the same as any other riot. According to the advocates of the method it is only by the repetition of experiments, with systematic variations, that a body of scientific knowledge can be built up and social psychological theories effectively tested.

Countless experiments were conducted through the 1960s in which volunteer subjects (usually students) were informed about a (usually) fictitious 'stranger's' attitudes, or his/her ethnic origin or religious affiliation, or were shown photographs of a physically attractive or unattractive person, and asked how much they thought they would like the other, or whether or not they would like to meet him/her. In the great majority of such experiments subjects never interacted face to face with anyone, except the experimenter. The advantages of this approach to research seemed considerable. In a real life encounter it is usually impossible to know exactly what it is about the other person that makes us like or dislike them, since we are faced with a whole mass of varied items of information, all at once: appearance, clothing, gestures and movements, speech style, even bodily odours; perhaps the person may also express opinions and attitudes. As Method Box 5.1 indicates, a series of laboratory experiments, by varying these 'ingredients' of the stranger in a systematic way, enables the researcher to explore the relative contributions of each to the subject's judgement of 'like' or 'dislike'. Among the most frequently repeated findings of such experiments are that physical attractiveness is of great significance in encounters with *any* stranger, and not only when boy meets girl; that we like strangers who appear similar to ourselves in attitudes, and the more similarity the better we like them; and that the most powerful of all the determinants of liking for a stranger is evidence that the stranger likes and approves of *us*.

As Method Box 5.1 also shows, laboratory experiments possess another valuable asset in the investigation of interpersonal attraction: they allow the experimenter to specify which factor causes what. Say we were to find, after a simple study where we interviewed a number of pairs of friends, that they were very similar across a range of attitudes, much more similar than pairs of people drawn at random. The really interesting question for a psychologist, and one which such a study could *not* answer, is which caused which—the friendship, or the similarity? Did the discovery of important shared viewpoints draw these people together in the first place, or were they originally attracted for other reasons but became similar as they exchanged attitudes and opinions during the development of their friendship? Each possible sequence has a sound basis in social psychological theory. The laboratory experiment aims to solve this causality problem quite straightforwardly. The experimenter explicitly and carefully controls the level of attitude similarity. One group of subjects may be presented with a 'stranger' who agrees with 80 per cent of their attitudes on a set of topics, a second group with a stranger similar to them on 50 per cent of their attitudes, while yet a third group 'encounters' a person who agrees with them on only 20 per cent of their opinions. If subsequent liking for the stranger varies directly with level of similarity (the most similar stranger best liked, the least similar least liked) then the experimenter can conclude that similarity produced the liking and not the other way around. Also, by controlling and standardizing all other possibly interfering factors, such as duration of exposure to the 'stranger', and the personalities of the subjects (this is achieved by assigning subjects at random to the various experimental groups), the experimenter can feel reasonably confident that it is attitude similarity, and not some other factor, that produced the liking response by subjects.

Notwithstanding the apparent advantages of the laboratory experiment over other methods, by the early 1970s many social psychologists working on friendship had become disenchanted with the approach. A few, such as Theodore Newcomb, had been using other methods of investigating relationships for several decades, and during the 1970s his example was followed by a growing number of other investigators.

Profile 5.1   Theodore Newcomb (1903–)

His Life

Born in the American Midwest Theodore Newcomb spent a brief period training for the religious ministry before going on to study psychology and he obtained his Ph. D. from Columbia Teachers' College in 1929. In the early 1930s he worked for a time as a union organizer and agitator; a political radical throughout his career, Newcomb was a leader in the academic movement against the US involvement in the Vietnam War in the 1960s. During the mid-1930s he conducted a study of attitude formation and change among students at Bennington College, where he taught; an important landmark in social psychological research, this study was conducted over a period of years, and related attitudes and values held by the students to their popularity and social status within the student body. After working for the US government during the Second World War, Newcomb took a post at the University of Michigan at Ann Arbor, where he remained for the rest of his career. He believed strongly that social psychology could be and ought to be applied to the resolution of social problems; in that, as in other aspects of his work, Newcomb was decades ahead of his time.

His work

In the 1950s Newcomb began his work on the acquaintance process which for over a decade stood as a unique contribution to the field: taking a group of complete strangers, Newcomb gave them a house to live in and observed the development of their relationships over a period of several months, and traced the changes in their attitudes and perceptions as relationships waxed and waned. The study was repeated a year later, with essentially similar findings: Newcomb observed that people were more likely to become attracted to those who shared their general attitudes and values, but that it was friendship itself that led to development of similar attitudes towards other people in the house. Perhaps the most interesting finding was that people consistently overestimated the extent of their similarity to those they liked. Newcomb explained these results as products of a tendency toward seeing social relationships in a balanced or orderly way—we see liking and agreement as going together, and both our perceptions and our social choices are influenced accordingly.

His importance

Newcomb had little time for laboratory experimentation; he was always interested in social processes as they unfolded in natural contexts, and in relating what went on in people's social lives to what went on 'in their heads'. His insistence that research should be directed at real life relationships in all their daunting complexity has encouraged and inspired contemporary social psychologists who are steadily developing and improving their methods and measures with that objective in mind.

Further reading

Newcomb, T. M (1961). *The Acquaintance Process*. New York: Holt; Newcomb, T. M. (1978). 'The Acquaintance Process: Looking Mainly Backward. *Journal of Personality and Social Psychology* 36, pp. 1075–83.

Attacks on the usefulness of the laboratory for research in friendship came on two fronts. On the one hand the limitations of the method for understanding events over time were pointed out; how could a procedure which exposed people to a stranger for such a brief period tell us anything worth knowing about the day-by-day growth of a personal relationship? A second onslaught from another quarter sought to attack the experiment on its home ground, the encounter with a stranger. How do we know, the critics asked, that information about attitudes is actually exchanged by strangers at first encounter? Perhaps this kind of relatively personal information is normally divulged much later on in the development of a friendship; if that is the case, it is of little theoretical or practical value to investigate the supposed effects of attitude similarity at a stage of acquaintance when such information is usually not available.

The advocates of experimentation have replied to these critiques, to some effect, but the emphasis of research into friendship has changed decisively in the past decade, away from experimental encounters with strangers and towards the study of real relationships over time. A parallel development has been a growing interest in the observation and recording of friendship activities, the small change of daily life; debates about the relevance of experiments to 'real life' revealed a vast degree of ignorance of such mundane but important details.

From Attraction to Commitment: The Development of Friendship

In the early 1970s a number of investigators, most notably Murstein in the USA (Murstein 1970) and Duck in Britain (Duck 1973), suggested that friendships develop through a fixed sequence of stages, much as other psychologists had suggested that a child's capacities for thought proceed by a regular series of steps. Each stage of friendship development has its own characteristic concerns. Murstein proposed that for some time after first encounter we are mainly influenced by the other person's external characteristics: their physical appearance, style of interaction, and so forth. If each person finds the other sufficiently attractive at this stage, the relationship moves on to the second step, in which the main focus of interest is the other person's attitudes and values *vis-à-vis* one's own. If each person proves satisfactorily similar to the other—and the discovery and testing of such similarity may take some time—then the friendship proceeds to the final stage of development, in which each participant evaluates the other as a potential friend in a very practical sense: can each partner make the necessary changes in life-style to accommodate the new relationship? Is the other capable of fulfilling the role requirements of friendship, such as loyalty, toler-ance, trust, and commitment? Murstein suggested that it is at this stage of establishing the compatibility of behaviours, habits, and preferences that many potentially intimate relationships fail to make the grade, and either remain as mere casual acquaintanceships or dwindle away.

Duck's model shares with that of Murstein an initial emphasis upon external appearance, followed by a concern with comparison of attitudes and values. Duck's proposed third stage, however, envisages a progressively more precise and specific evaluation by each partner of the other's fundamental ways of looking at the world and interpreting other people and events. In Duck's view the basic goal of friendship is the confirmation and reinforcement of self-esteem, through intimate association with a person (or persons) who shares one's own basic ways of making sense of things and under-standing the world we live in.

Duck's and Murstein's 'stage' theories are not necessarily in com-petition with each other. It may well be that a concern with role com-patibility operates in conjunction with a fine-grained analysis of the way in which the other person sees the world; indeed, the two pro-posed processes may facilitate each other. A degree of research sup-port has been found for both Murstein's and Duck's models, and also for other alternative approaches, but a great deal remains to be done before researchers can claim to understand the basic dynamics of a developing friendship. An increasing number of investigators are following Newcomb's early example, and conducting 'longitud-inal' studies of relationships, that is, observing and measuring friendships' progress over an extended time period. Such studies are laborious, expensive, and fraught with difficulties, but none the less indispensable.

Friendship Skills

An approach to the development of friendship which has begun to attract a considerable volume of interest among social psychologists concentrates on the social skills involved in the achievement and maintenance of a close personal relationship. The idea that friendship may be (at least in part) the product of a set of abilities and performance skills, just like any other practical achievement or complex task, is particularly appealing to those psychologists interested in helping people with relationship problems. If failure to attract or to keep friends is a matter of faulty interpersonal technique, then perhaps many such difficulties can be remedied, and people's lives enriched accordingly, by a training programme which helps the person to eliminate unattractive and discouraging mannerisms and to acquire more acceptable behaviours.

Profile 5.2   Steve Duck (1946-)

His life

The other profiles in this book have focused on some of the founding figures of the social sciences; by definition they are not typical. Steve Duck has been included as representative of contemporary social scientists. Born in 1946 in Keynsham, Avon, Duck read psychology at Oxford University and obtained his Ph. D. in social psychology from Sheffield University in 1971. In 1973 he joined the psychology department at the University of Lancaster, and in 1985 moved to the University of Iowa.

His work

The work of Steve Duck exemplifies well the approach of the 'second generation' of friendship researchers, taking the field out of its obsession with the laboratory that characterized the 1960s, and in a sense taking up and developing further the kinds of ideas and methods pioneered by Newcomb and very few others in the 1950s. An early interest in the vexed question of the relationship between personality similarity and friendship led into an exploration of how friendships might change as they develop. This work resulted in his three-stage model of friendship development already described, and in several series of studies designed to test and expand the model. Duck's work has been characterized by a very broad and flexible use of methods: interviews, questionnaires, role playing, laboratory studies, and long-term diary studies have been directed at different aspects of personal relationships.

In recent years Duck has extended his interest to the area of relationship breakdown and dissolution; he proposed in 1982 a four-stage model of dissolution which integrates processes operating within the minds of the participants, interactions between the two partners in the dissolving relationship, and interactions between the pair and the surrounding network of parents, children, and other friends. More recently still he has come to work on the repair of relationships in difficulties, which emphasizes the importance of tailoring attempts at repair to the particular stage of breakdown or dissolution the relationship has reached.

His importance

Duck has played a leading role in a drive to broaden and to internationalize the study of personal relationships, to make researchers aware of what is going on in other cultures and countries and in other branches of social science. To this end he has been the prime mover in establishing a series of international conferences, and in setting up the Journal of Social and Personal Relationships, which publishes work in friendship and intimate relationships generally across a range of social science disciplines.

Further reading

Duck, S. (1983). *Friends, For Life*. Brighton: Harvester Press.

Whilst this approach seems to be inadequate on its own to explain friendship development, there is a good deal of evidence that interpersonal skills are important, and also that they can be improved by systematic training. When two people interact, be they strangers or friends, many aspects of their behaviour are potentially rewarding or punishing to each other; as a general principle, we will tend to continue interacting with a person who pleases and rewards us, and avoid one who discourages or hurts us. The skills of acquaintance, it would seem, are therefore of two main kinds: the ability correctly to decode the signals others are sending, and the ability to modify one's own behaviour accordingly, so as to avoid unnecessary hurt and provide rewards to the other person.

The volume of information transmitted in even the briefest social interaction can be enormous: I am referring here to body movements of various kinds: facial expressions, eye movements, gestures, bodily orientation, and distance; to what is said (the verbal content); and, often more important, *how* it is said; tone of voice, speech rate, loudness, and various mannerisms. A great deal of evidence has accumulated over the last twenty years which attests to the crucial importance of such signals in the regulation and pacing of encounters, the expression of moods and emotional states, and also, of central relevance to the area of friendship, in conveying affection and approval, dislike, and contempt (for a very perceptive and readable survey of this work see Bull 1983).

Most people are probably reasonably proficient in handling such communications, at least within their own cultural enviroment; there is, incidentally, evidence of great cross-cultural differences in the meanings of such signals. To the extent, however, that a person has failed to learn the appropriate skills, or has learnt inappropriate behaviours, his or her chances of attracting a potential friend, or of coping with the complex work of maintaining and nurturing an existing relationship, are likely to be impaired. Social skills training may help such a person to express his or her feelings more clearly and comprehensibly, and to recognize and identify the meanings underlying others' behaviours more effectively.

The aspect of friendship skill which has received perhaps the most systematic attention from researchers in recent years is the process of self-disclosure; some writers (e.g. Jourard 1971) have claimed that it is the single most important element in the development of a relationship.

Concept Box 5.2 Self-disclosure

Self-disclosure refers to the things we tell others about ourselves; it may be relatively trivial (our favourite type of beer or ice-cream flavour), more personal (our political preferences or attitudes toward a third person), or very intimate (something in our past that we are deeply ashamed of, or a hitherto secret fantasy or wish). All friendship researchers see self-disclosure as an important aspect of friendship development; this isn't surprising when one considers the variety of functions that self-disclosure can serve. By disclosing we indicate trust in our partner; by responding positively and supportively to his or her disclosures, we convey both our affection and respect for our friend and appreciation of the trust reposed in us. Disclosure to a close friend can provide relief from pent-up anxieties, and may elicit advice and guidance towards the solution of our problems. Finally, and by no means least, self-disclosure can

constitute a strategic or tactical device by which we present ourselves in a manner best designed to win our partner's sympathy or
admiration.

Self-disclosure questionnaires, on which friends indicate the
kinds of topics typically discussed, are the usual method of studying
this kind of friendship activity. There are problems in such research:
people may not accurately recall all of their self-disclosing behaviours, and the people studied may not always agree on what consti-
tutes 'superficial' or 'intimate' topics.

In addition, because self-disclosure is by definition verbal, and
thus relatively easily recalled and observed, there may be a tendency to overestimate its true importance; people can learn a great
deal about each other via non-verbal signals, and not all relationships (or all cultures) go in for high levels of soul-baring.

These reservations aside, however, a good deal of evidence points
to the importance of self-disclosure, especially in the early stages of
a relationship's development, and also to the requirement for skill in
managing such disclosures. One person's revealing too much, too
soon, especially if the information is negative, can arouse anxiety
and precipitate withdrawal by the hearer. On the other hand, failing
to reciprocate appropriate levels of intimacy is also likely to retard
or stifle relationship development.

Another aspect of social skills to attract the attention of
researchers in recent years concerns how couples conduct their arguments. The main assumption underlying work in this area is that
periodic conflicts are inescapable in any close relationship; there are
so many forces in play within a friendship, and impinging upon it
from outside, that clashes are inevitable. For example, one partner's
desires or plans may conflict with those of the other; sometimes individual needs, such as the urge to succeed in a career, may appear to
be incompatible with the functioning of the relationship itself. Add
to this the common fact that outsiders (other friends, children, in-
laws) have an influence upon the lives of persons in a relationship
and that these influences will frequently be in competition with each
other.

Some researchers in marital relationships are convinced that the
best single means of predicting whether or not a marriage will
succeed or fail is to look at how the partners handle their differences
and disputes, even *before* they get married. Research has also begun
to identify some of the features of productive conflict, which leads to

some kind of solution, as compared with destructive conflict, which serves mainly to antagonize the contestants even further. It is also becoming clear that the complete absence of open conflict is more likely to indicate a dead or empty relationship than a genuinely harmonious partnership. Some workers in the area of marital dysfunction have begun a systematic examination of ways of helping people with relationship problems to bring their conflicts into the open, and deal with them constructively, avoiding mutually harrowing, circular, and unresolvable personal acrimony.

Characteristics of Friendships

We have looked in some detail at how social psychologists study friendships, and at the processes and skills involved in developing a personal relationship; we now turn to examine some aspects of the way in which established friendships actually operate and function, following a rather artificial but useful convention in psychology and focusing first on overt behaviours and activities, then on cognitions (thoughts, judgements, expectancies) and finally on affect (feelings and emotions).

Friendship behaviours

Friends tend to spend a good deal of time together, and to seek out each other's company in preference to that of others. It may seem strange, therefore, that social psychologists have only recently become interested in examining in detail what friends do together. Robert Hinde, an eminent British researcher into animal behaviour and child development, who has recently turned his attention to the study of personal relationships, has been critical of this neglect (Hinde 1979). One of his main arguments is that the development of adequate theories of friendship depends to a large extent upon the availability of an adequate accumulation of basic descriptive data, such as exist in the areas of animal behaviour and developmental psychology. There is a wide variety of approaches to this kind of investigation, ranging from diaries in which friends record salient events of the day to the use of electronic paging devices which participants in the study agree to wear; when the device emits its signal, at random intervals, the individual records whatever he or she happens to be doing at that moment. Another approach which has been widely used is the Activities' Questionnaire.

Method Box 5.2 Activities' Questionnaire

As its name indicates, this is a set of standardized questions about their activities which friends complete, usually individually, and usually over a set period of time. In a sense it resembles a diary, although it has the advantage of being more structured: the Activities' Questionnaire directs the participant to answer specific queries, rather than allowing him or her to write about events at will, as in a conventional diary. There is, of course, a corresponding drawback to this structured approach; it reduces the potential contribution of the participant's insight and intuition, and the answers will only be as good as the questions the investigator decides to ask. The main advantage of the Activities' Questionnaire over the diary, however, is that because it is structured and standardized, participants' responses can be directly compared, one with another.

One type of questionnaire now widely used and adapted is the Rochester Interaction Record (RIR), a device developed in 1977 at the University of Rochester in New York by Ladd Wheeler and John Nezlek (see Wheeler and Nezlek 1977). In their initial investigation the RIR was used to compare the interaction patterns of young adult males and females, something which had not previously been done. Each participant completed an RIR form for every two-person interaction of longer than ten minutes' duration that they engaged in over a two-week period; forms were completed at the end of each day. For each interaction the form required the following information: date; time of day; duration; with whom; who initiated the interaction; location; nature of the interaction (conversation, work, date, etc.); how intimate it was; and how satisfying it was. Subsequent users of the RIR method have adapted both the questions and the procedures to their own particular purposes.

Most of the information uncovered by instruments such as this is unsurprising and routine, but by no means all the things friends do are so easily predictable from intuition or 'common sense'. Mundane or not, it is important to record details such as the topics friends talk about, the size and composition of friends' social networks, who visits whom and how often, and which partner takes the decisions on how they will spend the evening. Only thus can investigators compare one type of friendship with another, and examine differences in activity with sex and age of participants, differences from one stage of a relationship to another, and variations in social class, and in ethnic and regional patterns of friendship behaviour. Without such fine-grained knowledge there is always a risk that theories of friendship will be unduly influenced by the theorist's own intuitions and life experiences, and by his or her philosophical or ideological predilections.

A broader perspective on friendship behaviour is taken by researchers whose main interest is in how established relationships regulate themselves. You will remember that in the section on friendship skills we looked briefly at conflict in relationships, and pointed out that conflicting forces are always likely to be operating to a greater or lesser extent in any friendship. One approach to understanding how such mutually opposing forces are handled and regulated is that of equity theory.

Concept Box 5.3 Equity Theory

Originally proposed by Stacy Adams in 1965 (see Adams 1965), equity theory was reformulated in the 1970s by Elaine Hatfield, then of the University of Wisconsin, and her co-workers, and has been extensively applied to the explanation of aspects of personal relationships. Equity theory is based on the assumption that human behaviour is essentially *hedonistic*, that is, that we are primarily motivated to seek pleasure and avoid pain. However, in order to ensure the maximum possible amount of satisfaction in social life, and to avoid chaos, societies evolve and enforce rules of fairness which regulate our behaviour, and these rules are passed on from one generation to the next. The most important of these rules, according to the theory, is equity: that rewards and contributions should be *proportionate*, so that those who contribute a lot should get a lot in return, and those who contribute little should receive little. Accordingly, the theory proposes that we strive for equity in our personal relationships, and that we are distressed (i.e. feel resentful or guilty) if our relationship is inequitable. This distress motivates us to resolve the situation either practically (by changing the balance of contributions and rewards in the direction of greater equity) or psychologically (by convincing ourselves that things really are fair, after all). Since people are basically hedonists (pleasure-seekers), the theory proposes that the partner who is under-benefitted, and hence resentful, will try to change the actual relationship, whilst the

over-benefitted partner, who feels guilty, will prefer to reinterpret
the situation so that he or she can continue to enjoy the benefits *and*
feel good about it too. The stage is therefore set for a certain amount
of struggle! From the point of view of equity theory, relationships as
they develop and change are constantly establishing and often
reformulating rules of fairness, whereby responsibilities and chores
are allocated and rewards shared out. Changing circumstances,
such as the birth of a child, or a partner becoming unemployed or
changing jobs, will make changes in the rules necessary so as to
maintain equity. This calls for a degree of flexibility in people that
may not always be forthcoming; however, the extent to which a relationship can evolve and maintain systems of functioning which are
perceived as equitable by both partners is an indication that a relationship is likely to prosper and to have high levels of participant
satisfaction. The theory sees breakdown of a relationship as a consequence of prolonged failure to establish such an equitable system of
regulation.

There are problems with equity theory; in particular, as equity is
in the eye of the beholder it is difficult to measure, and the immense
variety of social 'rewards' makes it hard to apply the theory to any
particular relationship. None the less there is a good deal of support
for the theory, and it has the great merit of trying to explain the
development, maintenance, and decline of relationships, with one
and the same set of theoretical principles.

Friendship cognitions

You will recall how Newcomb in his landmark study of the acquaintance process (see Profile 5.1) found that friends tended to overestimate the extent to which their own liking for another was
reciprocated, and also the extent to which friends shared their own
attitudes and opinions. These findings have been repeated in many
investigations since, and whereas Newcomb explained them as part
of our tendency to see social relations in as 'balanced' or harmonious
a way as possible, others interpret these distortions as an example of
what social psychologists call a self-serving bias: a tendency to interpret our friends' actions and utterances so as to reflect as well as possible upon ourselves. These aspects of friendship have fascinated
many researchers in the area: our perceptions, judgements, and
memories of events within a relationship constitute an almost limit-
less store of potential riches for such investigators to explore. In

everyday speech we say of our friends that we 'know them well', but research suggests that this knowledge is often patchy and highly selective. Whilst there is some excuse for gross errors in our perceptions of strangers, one might argue, surely repeated contacts with friends should gradually eliminate such misjudgements, and produce a more and more accurate impression of their character, preference, and abilities? Quite apart from the ever-present tendency to see what we want to see (the self-serving bias), there is some reason to believe that the acquisition of accurate knowledge of our friends is a chancy business. Human information-processing systems seem designed to simplify and to select; to attend to vivid and striking events and ignore the often more important slow and subtle changes; to reach quick decisions on incomplete information, and then to stick to those assessments even in the face of new and contrary evidence. In fairness to the human perceiver, though, the task of 'knowing' one's friend isn't as easy as it may at first appear. We do not usually have access to our friend's moment-by-moment thought processes, nor do we normally know as much about the friend's life history as he or she does. Our partner's self-disclosures to us are also likely to distort matters: a friend may shy away from explicitly stating his or her disagreements with us, but is likely to emphasize instances of agreement and harmony. It is not surprising, then, that in the important business of trying to understand our friend we are often likely to construct images and interpretations which bear little resemblance to the version of events which the friend would have produced.

The picture is not, of course, by any means entirely discouraging. There is good evidence that we can be very proficient indeed at 'reading' the non-verbal signals emitted by our friends, and it may also be the case that we are on occasion capable of explaining and understanding a friend's behaviour more accurately and comprehensively than the friend can—although he or she may not thank us for the enlightenment!

Friendship feelings

In the eyes of the person in the street, friendship is essentially about feelings. Behaviours and cognitions may all have their place, but what makes close friendship different from any other kind of human relationship is its high content of affection and emotional involvement. For the psychologist, however, emotion has proved a methodological and theoretical can of worms, a topic of enormous complexity and elusiveness. Even if one restricts the scope of attention to the apparently most clear-cut aspect of emotion in relationships, namely sexual love, there are as yet unresolved problems in sorting out the respective roles of physiological and psychological processes. 'Love' may, in fact, encompass a number of rather distinct phenomena: romantic attraction, altruistic commitment, conjugal love, sexual passion, each with its own unique pattern of feelings, cognitions, and behaviours. A particular relationship may contain several of these 'varieties' at any given time.

As yet, theory and research in the emotional aspects of personal relationships are in their infancy. The romantic love phenomenon has probably received more attention than any other aspect; it appears to involve high levels of physiological arousal, intense absorption in and idealization of the partner, high incidences of fantasy, day-dreaming, restlessness, and alternate states of euphoria and dejection. Writers are generally agreed that the onset of romantic love is often sudden, and that it does not usually develop out of a pre-existing close friendship. Surprisingly, opposition from outsiders (parents, other friends) can actually help to intensify romantic love, as it sustains arousal, increases a sense of unity in the couple, and promotes fantasy.

Ellen Berscheid, who has led social psychological enquiry into emotion in relationships, has pointed out (Berscheid 1983) that by its very nature romantic love, like the state of 'happiness', must be a short-lived phenomenon. High levels of physiological arousal cannot be maintained for a long period; regular sexual gratification and increased familiarity with the loved one inevitably reduce it. In addition, idealization of the partner, day-dreaming, and fantasy are bound to fade as familiarity and predictability grow. Romantic love may, however, with care and skill, be transformed into the more pragmatic 'conjugal' love, a less exalted but more sustainable condition which emphasizes contentment rather than happiness, as well as interpersonal trust, tolerance, and equity. From this point of view, the popular ideology that advocates romantic love as a basis for long-term commitment, and offers 'happiness' in relationship as a life goal to be striven for is at best misguided, and at worst pernicious.

Social psychologists have never claimed that their 'scientific' approach is the only road to understanding the complex and changing phenomena we call, collectively, 'friendship'. Artists, dramatists, poets, and novelists have also contributed, often in much more vivid and memorable style than that of most psychological writers! Psychologists will, however, assert that the scientific perspective offers a valid and promising route to at least a partial comprehension of these mysteries, to the ultimate benefit of everyone.

References

Adams, J. S. (1965). 'Inequity in Social Exchange'. In L. Berkowitz (ed.). *Advances in Experimental Social Psychology* 2. New York: Academic Press.

Berscheid, E. (1983). Emotion. In H. Kelley *et al. Close Relationships*. New York: W. H. Freeman.

Bloom, B. L., S. J. Asher, and S. W. White (1978). 'Marital Disruption As a Stressor: A Review and Analysis. *Psychological Bulletin* 85, pp. 867–94.

Bull, P. (1983). *Body Movement and Interpersonal Communication*. Chichester: Wiley.

Duck, S. (1973). *Personal Relationships and Personal Constructs*. Chichester: Wiley.

Hinde, R. L. (1979). *Towards Understanding Relationships*. London: Academic Press.

Jourard, S. (1971). *Self-disclosure*. New York: Wiley.

Murstein, B. I. (1970). Stimulus-value-role: A Theory of Marital Choice. *Journal of Marriage and the Family* 32, pp. 465–81.

Wheeler, L. and J. Nezlek (1977). Sex Differences in Social Participation. *Journal of Personality and Social Psychology* 35, pp. 742–54.

Further Reading

An excellent brief survey of research in friendship and close relationships generally is Steve Duck (1983). *Friends for Life*. Brighton: Harvester Press. More advanced treatment is provided in two other recent texts, H. H. Kelley *et al.* (1983). *Close Relationships*. New York: Freeman and S. Duck and D. Perlman (eds.) (1985). *Understanding Personal Relationships*. London: Academic Press.

Among the vast of array introductions to the general field of social psychology, two useful books are: Leonard Berkowitz (1980). *A Survey of Social Psychology* 2nd edn. New York: Holt and Robert Baron and Donn Byrne (1984). *Social Psychology* 4th edn. Boston: Allyn & Bacon.

6 The Limits of Social Science

The early chapters in this book have concentrated on explaining social scientific ways of thinking and hence by implication on the accomplishments of social science. It is appropriate to conclude by examining the limits of social science. One reason for doing this is to enable the reader to have realistic expectations about the disciplines involved. On the one hand they are sometimes attacked because critics believe that social science has contributed very little to knowledge—that 'it's all common sense'. On the other hand some people believe that social scientists can explain an enormous variety of problems and that their findings represent some kind of universal truth.

The real position of social science lies between these two extremes. Social science can change the way we see and interpret the world. It can explain a good deal of human behaviour and its findings can help to improve social policy. But, on the other hand, there are huge areas of life where social science can say little of consequence. Explanations which seem adequate now will not be so in a few years and some social science 'laws' do not justify this title. Consequently readers of social science books—including this one—should have a sceptical approach. Who says so? How do we know? What is the evidence?—these are the questions that discriminating readers should ask themselves.

Limits Arising From the Individual Social Scientist

The first limit is obvious; we would all be able to understand more if we were cleverer. Even the greatest minds cannot solve all problems and so they make errors and false judgements. Our ideas inevitably reflect the age in which we live, and social scientists no less than the rest of society are imbued with the ideas which surround them. Even the most progressive thinkers cannot avoid this. Thus Marx, who in so many ways challenged the ideas of his time, had views which seem obnoxious today. On women he wrote 'Women are funny creatures—even those endowed with much intelligence', and 'Women plainly always need to be controlled' (McLellan 1976, p. 323, 357). On race his views are even more unacceptable today. Writing about a French socialist called Lassalle Marx wrote, 'It is now quite clear to me that, as shown by the shape of his head and the growth of his hair, that he is descended from the negroes who joined the flight of Moses from Egypt (unless his mother or grandfather on his father's side were crossed with a nigger). This union of Jew and German on a negro foundation was bound to produce something out of the ordinary. The importunity of the fellow is also negroid' (McLellan 1976, p. 322).

Just as Marx's attitudes were affected by his environment, so do the ideas and theories of all social societies grow out of the times in which they live. Thus Aristotle could not have created Keynes's theories because they developed in the context of an advanced industrial society.

Moreover there is so much to learn that no individual can understand more than a small part of social science. Thus almost all social scientists learn their 'trade' by taking a course at an institution of higher education. A typical course will contain several subjects in the first year—some economics, some sociology, some politics, for example—but by the final year of the course the student will be concentrating on just one area. If the student wishes to continue into postgraduate studies the area of investigation will be more specialized, so that most researchers in social science would only claim expertise in one part of one social science discipline.

However, problems overlap disciplines. Understanding topics such as work or race relations requires the contributions of several disciplines. Few people have the ability to master more than one discipline so that the contribution of any one individual will immediately be limited and any investigation will be approached through the blinkers of a particular discipline. This difficulty can, in principle at least, be overcome by the formation of interdisciplinary teams, but in practice these may be expensive to set up and cooperation between individuals with different approaches may be difficult to achieve.

Social scientists face a difficulty not usually found in the physical sciences: that of values. The social and political values of a physicist studying the structure of the atom will not directly affect his or her work, but a sociologist studying housing may well have strong views about policy in this area and these views may affect the research.

A real example will illustrate the difficulty. Three researchers, Lewin, Lippitt, and White (1939), wanted to examine the effects of democratic and authoritarian group structures on behaviour. They organized an experiment in which eleven-year-old boys were divided into groups. In some groups the supervisor was an authoritarian leader who called the boys together and gave out orders. In the democratic group the supervisor became a member of the group and the boys themselves decided the activities. The results showed that more was accomplished in the democratic group where there was also a lot of communication, more suggestions, and more affection for the supervisor. In the authoritian group activities were formal, there was apathy, and some hostility towards other group members.

The implications *seem* clear. Democratic forms of organization work better than authoritarian ones. However, the result must be accepted with caution. The year was 1939, the world was dividing into democratic and authoritarian alliances; one of the researchers was a refugee from Hitler and all of them believed in democracy. In other words, however careful the researchers may have been there was a considerable chance that their beliefs would affect the results.

In a few cases researchers have believed so strongly that they know the truth that they have deliberately manipulated their findings. A leading British psychologist called Burt used intelligence tests to show the importance of heredity as opposed to environment. Many years later it was shown that he had probably 'adjusted' the figures to get the result that he wanted.

These are specific examples of a very broad problem. Individual researchers *do* have opinions and the problems they examine are often related to their views. Indeed there is some controversy in social science as to whether it is possible to have *any* value-free social science.

Researchers' expectations may affect their results. Spectators at a football match will have quite different opinions about an incident if they support opposing sides, because they will see what they expect to see. In the same way researchers in social science will often obtain the results they expect. The most notable example of this is probably an experiment by Rosenthal and Fode (1963). Sixty rats were divided at random into two groups. Students were asked to measure the length of time it took the rats to run through a maze to search for food—a kind of intelligence test for rats. Each rat was given fifty chances to learn the route through the maze. Although the groups' were identical, one group of students was told that its rats were dull and the other that its group was bright. The students timed the rats. At the end of the experiment the students who believed their rats were bright reported much faster times for their rats than the students who believed that their rats were dull. This may have occurred because the 'bright' rats received more affectionate handling and therefore ran faster. Moreover those who believed their rats were bright also felt that their rats were pleasant and likeable. Thus student expectations were fulfilled; they saw what they expected to see.

Similar criticisms have been made of other researchers. Margaret Mead's work was discussed in the chapter on the family, but a later anthropologist visted the South Seas and investigated some of the tribes. He came to the conclusion that Mead had been misled because she wanted to find evidence of societies where men's and women's roles were not determined by their sex so that she only saw activities which would support her ideas (Freeman 1983). It is only fair to add that this later writer may consciously or unconsciously have been looking for evidence to attack Mead, and that the balance of opinion among anthropologists seems generally to support Mead. We saw too, in the first chapter, that social scientists differ in the underlying perspectives they adopt. The choice that individual social scientists make between those contrasting perspectives—often unconsciously—may well be determined by their personal ideologies and perhaps their education, rather than on the basis of objectively considered and rational thought.

Words As a Limitation

Words can be chosen which will cause the reader to more or less favourably inclined to an argument. One of the basic problems analysed by economists is how resources should be allocated—since no society can produce everything that people would like, what should be produced? One approach to this problem is to leave it to market forces of supply and demand. In other words if consumers are willing to pay for something, it will be produced if manufacturers

can make a profit (an alternative system would be for the government to decide what to produce). The system of market forces has
many advantages and disadvantages which cause strong arguments.
Those who like the system write about 'free enterprise' rather than
'market forces' and criticize government 'interference' rather than
government 'intervention'. Words such as 'free enterprise' and
'interference' are not neutral; they influence the reader's thoughts
irrespective of the strength of the argument. Consciously or unconsciously social scientists, like advertisers, can use words to influence
attitudes.

Words present problems in other ways. When social scientists
want to find out something an obvious approach is to ask by using,
say, questionnaires or interviews. Here a prime difficulty is how to
phrase the questions so that the meaning is clear. For example, sup-
pose a researcher wished to discover if those with a lot of education
earned more than those with a little education. One way to approach
this problem would be to devise a questionnaire and ask people
about their earnings and education. This is quite difficult to do. For
example, do 'earnings' include overtime, or occasional earnings
from a second job, or back pay or bonuses? And how should the
amount of education be measured? Thus words are needed to find
out; but the choice of words to find out exactly what we want to
know may cause great problems.

These difficulties are repeated in many areas of social research.
Exactly what do we mean by 'poor housing'? What is a 'family'?
Sometimes the same word can cover such a wide range of behaviour
that it is almost meaningless. Thus 'crime' can cover anything from
parking a car in the wrong place or riding a bicycle without lights to
murder. If someone claims 'there is more crime now than there used
to be', it is not clear what is meant or how the statement could be
verified.

Another difficulty with words is that they do not always mean the
same thing to different people. In everyday life we talk about 'invest-
ing in a building society', yet to the economist the word 'investment'
has a fairly precise meaning that would exclude statements such as
the above. Instead economists would talk about 'saving in a building
society'. This specialized meaning given to words means that those
who do not know the 'language' may misunderstand what they read.
Indeed some writers use so much jargon that even specialists find
meanings difficult to understand. Yet it is impossible to express pre-

cise thoughts without using words (or mathematical symbols) in an exact way. Thus some jargon is inevitable.

Limits Arising From the Complexity of the Real World

Predictability is often considered the ultimate objective of scientific knowledge. Astronomers can predict the movement of the planets with great accuracy. Chemists can predict that if x atoms of one chemical combine with y atoms of another then z molecules of a compound will be formed. This ability to make precise predictions is seen by many people to be the most essential characteristic of 'science'. Yet even the most precise sciences have considerable limits; no physicist could predict where a balloon released from the top of Blackpool tower would land. And no one can say precisely where or when the next earthquake will occur or how much rain there will be next week.

In social science predictions can be made but they are frequently imprecise, vague, or surrounded by so many qualifications that they are of little use. One reason for this is that social science deals with an incredibly complex phenomenon—the behaviour of people in society. There are so many variables affecting the actions of humans that it is not surprising that predictions are inaccurate. As chapter 5 showed, social psychologists can forecast friendship formation in general, but they cannot forecast with certainty whether A will make friends with B. People make friends with those of similar interests—but sometimes opposites attract. They may be open to friendship one day, but feel ill on another and wish to be alone. Moreover the empirical laws established by social scientists may be valid for only a relatively brief historical period. Changing societal variables many fundamentally alter the nature and hence the determinants of friendship, for example. And an analysis which is relevant to one society may be quite inapplicable to another. One reason for this is that people in different societies are socialized so that they behave in different ways. This makes it difficult to make generalizations about people as a whole.

People sometimes seem to behave in irrational ways. Economists usually predict that when prices are rising people will save less and spend more. The reason is that any money saved will buy less in the future. This prediction has proved accurate in many countries at many different times. However, in the inflation in the UK in the 1970s people saved *more* as prices rose. The reason is unknown; perhaps they tried to maintain the value of their savings as the future seemed unsure. Whatever the reason economic predictions were inaccurate because people behaved differently than in the past.

Moreover human beings are capable of learning and changing their behaviour. An atom of oxygen will always act like an atom of oxygen, but John Smith may behave quite differently next week to the way he did last week because he has learned from his experiences.

A related problem in social science is that people may behave differently *because* of the work of the social scientists. If an economist predicts that the price of sugar will rise, then some people may buy extra sugar before it rises and this extra demand may force up the price. The prediction has changed the behaviour. Similarly opinion polls before an election which suggest that a particular party will win may encourage its supporters and discourage opponents so that the prediction changes the votes cast. In the same way it is possible that Marx's prediction that conflict between the classes would result in the overthrow of capitalism has not occurred because the prediction has alerted capitalists and encouraged them to take action such as the development of public welfare provision to forestall any revolution.

People may behave differently because they know they are under observation. One of the most famous investigations in social science illustrates this. A number of researchers under the direction of Mayo, from the Harvard Graduate School observed workers at the Hawthorne works of the General Electric Company in Chicago in the 1920s. They were trying to find out if productivity improved if material conditions such as lighting and heating were improved. They found that productivity did indeed increase.

They also discovered that productivity increased when material conditions were made worse! The researchers eventually concluded that the extra productivity had nothing to do with the material conditions, but occurred because of the interest shown in the workers. This result is usually called the Hawthorne effect: people under observation change their behaviour and respond to experimental conditions. The Hawthorne effects occurs in many areas of research. For example, a number of researchers have attempted to discover if different methods of teaching are better than others as measured by children's learning. However, the very act of observing teachers and children changes their behaviour so that greater learning may occur whatever the teaching method.

Social science models are a simplification of reality since the real world is too complex to be included in any model. This means that researchers must decide which variables are important and which can be omitted. In some cases this is easy—a geographer making a map of a town would include roads and important buildings such as post offices, but would find it easy to exclude lamp posts, trees, or other phenomena which would not help map users. In other cases deciding what to include or exclude is more difficult and important variables may be excluded. The truth is not waiting to declare itself and we often cannot know in advance which variables may be important and which can be excluded. Since many variables may be left in the model, a useful technique is to attempt to hold others constant and decide what will happen if only one varies. Thus a chemist may keep pressure constant and observe what happens to the volume of a gas when the temperature changes. In the social sciences this may be difficult to do because there are so many possible variables. For example, economists often try to predict the quantity of a good that will be bought. There are many variables which affect this—its price, the price of competing goods, changes in consumers' incomes, advertising, and so on. The economist may wish to forecast how much demand will fall if the price of the good rises. This is not easy to do because all the other variables will be changing and influencing how much consumers buy. Thus, if the price of a newspaper rises by a penny people may actually buy more if there is a sensational murder trial or if competing papers are on strike or the paper has a successful advertising campaign. The economist may attempt to isolate the effects of variables such as these, but it is not surprising if predictions are inaccurate.

One limit to the accuracy of social science arise because it deals with people and therefore moral considerations arise. A physicist can observe the behaviour of a steel rod under stress until it is destroyed but equivalent experiments are not possible in social science and consequently experiments on people are limited in scope.

A related limitation is that the physical sciences build up a body of knowledge by replicating experiments. If several researchers at different times and places repeat an experiment then its results will be generally accepted. In social science people's behaviour will vary over time and between societies so that it is difficult to replicate experiments and hence to corroborate or discredit theories which have been supported by some experimental evidence.

Limits Arising From Inadequate Data

Whilst scientific thinking is possible without quantification, it frequently does involve the use of numbers because these are needed to give precision and accuracy. This may create problems because accurate figures may not be available. Occasionally this is because it is in people's interest to manipulate the data. For example in the Nigerian elections of 1983 it was difficult to discover how many people were entitled to vote because there were allegations that people had been left off the electoral roll by political opponents. Thus it will never be possible to say precisely how many people were entitled to vote. Similarly statistics about levels and distribution of incomes are usually derived from income tax returns and are inaccurate because people try to minimize their reported incomes.

Sometimes people are reluctant or unwilling to supply information. Thus data on the racial/ethnic composition of society are limited because some people would object. In the preparations for the 1981 census in the UK it was at first agreed that a question on racial origin would be included, but this was later left off the form because of its political sensitivity. Another reason was the difficulty in framing questions—from what racial group is someone who was born in Britain whose father was of Scottish descent but born in Kenya and whose mother was from Hong Kong?

Questions of sensitivity and secrecy are often a problem to social scientists, particularly the political scientist. Many decisions are taken in secret and documents may be destroyed or locked away until many years after the event.

Even where data are available, they may not measure what is wanted. Psychologists may be interested in the extent of mental stress or mental illness; figures for the latter may be obtained—for example, for the number of patients entering mental hospital—such statistics, however, do not really measure the extent of mental illness; rather they measure the number of places available in mental hospitals and also changes in policy about whether mental patients should be treated in hospital or at home. Similarly, 'mental stress' could be measured by the use of proxies such as the number of prescriptions for tranquillizer drugs or the number of suicides. These may give some indication, but they do not measure mental stress directly or precisely. Consequently, statements by psychologists about the extent of mental stress can never be precise.

Similarly, crime statistics are inaccurate. In the first place much—perhaps most—crime is never notified to the police. If someone has a minor car accident the authorities may not be told; if a couple of drunks have a fight the police will usually not know; if a person has a small amount of money taken he may not bother to inform the police unless he wishes to claim insurance. Thus changes in the level of reported crime may measure the extent of people telling the police rather than changes in the number of crimes.

A specific example of the difficulties imposed by inadequacies of data is the research by two distinguished economists into the efficiency of British Secondary Education (Woodhall and Blaug 1968). The concept of efficiency is one which relates inputs to outputs. In the case of something like a furniture factory this is relatively easy to measure—inputs such as hours worked, quantity of materials and machines are used to produce outputs such as chairs and tables. In education the inputs are teachers and other staff, buildings and equipment, and also the value of student time. The output of education is presumably some kind of learning. Since they could not measure this directly, Woodhall and Blaug used a variety of proxy measures such as examination passes. They also used the length of education as a measure of output when in fact this is an input— student time is a resource used in the production of learning. For the record, the researchers found that productivity had fallen, but their research was fatally flawed by their inability to find a satisfactory measure of the output of education.

Conclusion

The focus of this book has been the ways of thinking and methods of investigation used by social scientists. Whilst we have not tried to give full descriptions of the methods used, we have tried to show the limitations involved whatever method is used. Whether they are building up mathematical models, setting up experiments, or asking questions, researchers are aware of the limitations of their work and the good ones make these clear when reporting the results.

Just as a doctor always loses the final battle because eventually the patient will die, so social scientists will never find universal truth.

Nevertheless human beings are curious; we want to find out, to know more. Social scientists are on a journey whose destination of ultimate truth will never be reached, but however difficult the voyage we can achieve the rewards of understanding more about society and perhaps help to improve it.

References

Freeman, D. (1983). *Margaret Mead and Samoa*. Harmondsworth: Penguin.

Lewin, K., R. Lippitt, and R. K. White (1939). 'Patterns of Aggressive Behaviour in Experimentally Created Social Climates'. *Journal of Social Psychology* 10, pp. 271–99.

McLellan, D. (1976). *Karl Marx*. London: Granada.

Rosenthal, R. and K. L. Fode (1963). 'The Effects of Experimental Bias on the Performance of Albino Rats'. *Behavioural Science*, pp. 183–9.

Woodhall, M. and M. Blaug (1968). 'Productivity Trends in British Secondary Education'. *Sociology of Education*.

Index